VICE & VIRTUE:
GRAMMAR AND POETICS TEXTBOOK
(WITH ANSWERS)

VICE & VIRTUE

GRAMMAR AND POETICS TEXTBOOK

WITH ANSWERS

Instruction and exercises in grammar and poetics
for students in the fourth to sixth grades by

WILLIAM D. WALTER

Wombley Press

© 2015 William D. Walter

No part of this book may be reproduced or used in any form or by any means without obtaining written permission from the publisher.

Student edition: ISBN 978-1-943939-34-3
With answers: ISBN 978-1-943939-35-0

CONTENTS

GRAMMAR AND PUNCTUATION   1

1   The Sentence   3
2   Nouns and Verbs   6
3   Linking Verbs   8
4   The Simple Subject and Verb   10
5   Helping Verbs and Main Verbs   12
6   Regular and Irregular Verbs   14
7   Voice   17
8   Subjunctive Mood   19
9   Nouns and Subject–Verb Agreement   21
10   Personal Pronouns (1)   25
11   Personal Pronouns (2)   29
12   Adjectives   32
13   Adverbs   35
14   Pronoun Agreement   37
15   Prepositions   39
16   Prepositional Phrases   40
17   Coordinating Conjunctions   43
18   Subordinating Conjunctions   46
19   Quotations (1)   50
20   Quotations (2)   54
21   Quotations (3)   57
22   Commas (1)   59

23 Commas (2) 62
24 Apostrophes (1) 64
25 Apostrophes (2) 66
26 Apostrophes (3) 67
27 Capitals 71
28 Titles 74
29 End Marks and Abbreviations 76
30 Run-ons 78
31 Semicolons 80
32 Comprehensive Review 83

POETRY AND POETICS 89

1 What a Poem Looks Like 91
2 The Language of Poetry 96
3 Figurative Language in Poetry 100
4 Irony and Oxymoron 103
5 Music in Poetry 106
6 Syllables 108
7 Stress 110
8 Examples of Music in Poetry 114
9 Scansion 117
10 Iamb 121
11 Greek Words in Poetry 124
12 Meter 126
13 Trochee 131
14 Spondee 132
15 Catalectic and Acatalectic 133
16 Anapestic 137
17 Dactylic 139
18 Stanza Forms and the Ballad 141

CONTENTS

19 The Sonnet   143
20 Euphony and Perfect Rhyme   146
21 Imperfect Rhyme   150
22 Alliteration   153
23 Masculine and Feminine Rhyme   156
24 Internal Rhyme and Caesura   160
25 Rhyme Schemes   163
26 Writing Music to Poetry   167
27 Narrative Poetry   170
28 Epic Poems   175
29 Lyric Poetry   179
30 Themes and Topics of Poetry   182
31 Enjambment and End Stop   187
32 Middle Ages and Renaissance   192
33 The Romantic Period   197
34 Victorian and Modern Poets   201
35 Writing Poetry   206
36 Review   208

WORKS CONSULTED   211

GRAMMAR AND PUNCTUATION

Grammar and Punctuation 1
The Sentence

What is a sentence? Perhaps you would be able to recognize one, but can't tell what one is. You should be able, however, to give a working definition: *A sentence is a group of words that has a complete subject and a predicate and expresses a complete thought.* The subject answers the question *who* or *what* the sentence is about. Sometimes there is more than one subject in a sentence. In such a case, we say that the sentence has a **compound subject**. The predicate part finishes the sentence and contains the verb. In the following sentence, the subject is underlined once and the predicate is underlined twice.

Example of a Sentence

Nelson and his family visited our family in July.

To find the complete subject, you ask, "Who or what is the sentence is about?" The answer to that question is *Nelson and his family* (underlined once). You will notice that the predicate *visited our family in July* (underlined twice) finishes the sentence and contains the verb *visited*. (A verb shows action or being. The words *jump, drive, roll, is,* and *am* are all verbs.) Notice that when they are together, the subject and predicate express a complete thought. Read the following and see if you can tell which one is a sentence.

(1) Made a shed in the backyard for his tools.
(2) Anna's sister sewed a dress.
(3) Because she was swimming downstream in the dirty river.
(4) At Ridley Creek State Park in the rain.
(5) Jonam working at the farm in Kimberton.

Were you able to tell that (2) expresses a complete thought, while the the others do not? It contains both a subject and predicate. The rest are fragments because they lack a complete subject, as in (1); a predicate, as in (5), or both, as in (4). It might seem that (3) contains a subject and a predicate, but it does not express a complete thought. Here is sentence (2) written again with the **complete subject** underlined once, and the **predicate** underlined twice:

(2) Anna's sister sewed a dress.

Exercise 1.1

Underline the subject of the sentence once and the predicate twice. Make sure that every word of the sentence is underlined. The first one has been done for you.

1. The lion roared inside its cage.
2. Tim's bicycle cost $500.
3. The huge boulder was rolling down the steep hill.
4. Bill found a ballpoint pen under the sofa.
5. Frankie's sailboat was freshly painted.
6. The supermarket clerk gave the girl a balloon.
7. Standing behind a tree, Joshua hid from his friends.
8. We awoke from the loud thunder.
9. The angry old man in the car yelled at the pedestrian.
10. I forgot to bag the mayonnaise at the store.

Exercise 1.2

After each of the following, write "F" if it is a fragment and "S" if it is a sentence. The first one has been done for you.

1. Outside the house.   F
2. Is giving a present for his birthday.   F
3. Samuel daydreamed in the backseat of the car.   S
4. Could John pay for the candy with his own money?   S

THE SENTENCE

5. Our blue van needed repair. S
6. To listen to music at the concert hall? F
7. Camping in a ragged tent on the hill. F
8. George's aunt from Idaho. F
9. Angry that his brother had taken his penknife without asking. F
10. The old woman recovered from her illness. S

Exercise 1.3

Sometimes a fragment has a subject and a verb but doesn't express a complete thought because it begins with a "dependent word." Dependent words include such words as *because, if, when, where, although, while, since, and, but, for, yet, or,* and *which*. Cross out the dependent words in the following fragments to make them sentences. The first one has been done for you.

1. ~~If~~ you took the bus this morning.
2. ~~When~~ it was evening and I went out on the empty beach.
3. ~~Although~~ Sam was not wealthy.
4. ~~Even though~~ he wasn't happy about the situation.
5. ~~While~~ Bob was studying and Mary was reading her book.
6. ~~Since~~ my friend Karen and I like to play the same games.
7. ~~While~~ I was eating my breakfast.
8. ~~And~~ George was a fast eater.
9. ~~Except that~~ he noticed even though you tried to hide it from him.
10. ~~Because~~ he was tired from swimming so long in the hot sun.

Grammar and Punctuation 2
Nouns and Verbs

There are almost one million words in the English language and yet all of them belong to one of eight parts of speech. They include nouns, pronouns, verbs, adjectives, adverbs, prepositions, conjunctions and interjections.

Dictionaries are useful in that they not only give a definition of a word, but also tell the part of speech. These parts of speech might be abbreviated: a noun may be indicated by the abbreviation *n.*, a verb by the abbreviation *v.*, a pronoun by the abbreviation *pron.*, and so on. Two of the largest families of words are the noun and the verb. Look below at the dictionary entry for the word *refuge*. Notice that its part of speech is indicated right next to the word.

> **refuge** /ˈrɛ.fjudʒ/ *n.* **1** : a safe place for anyone who is in danger **2** : any place or thing that gives quiet, rest or relief [from Latin *re-* away, back + *fugere* flee] *The family ran away from their country and sought ~ in the US.*

Nouns

A **noun** is a word that names a person, place, or thing. Sometimes the word does not name a thing that you can touch, taste, see, hear or smell. This kind of noun is called an **abstract noun**. Abstract nouns name ideas or feelings. All other nouns are called **concrete nouns**.

Examples of Nouns

Concrete	cousin, priest, sky, hill, blueberry, bone
Abstract	love, happiness, panic, trial, fun, society

Verbs

A **verb** is a word that describes an action, or a link between two words. If you can *do* it, it is an **action verb**. Words such as *sing, wash, pray,* and *lift* are all action verbs. You will learn about the **linking verbs** in a later section.

NOUNS AND VERBS

Exercise 2.1

Memorize the underlined definitions of a noun and a verb.

Exercise 2.2

Look up each of the following words in a dictionary, and write down its part of speech.

1. not   adverb
2. hasty   adjective
3. destroy   verb
4. trespass   noun
5. because   conjunction
6. ouch   interjection
7. distress   noun
8. himself   pronoun
9. clock   noun
10. of   preposition

Exercise 2.3

Underline the nouns (including proper names) once and the verbs twice. The first one has been done for you.

1. <u>Anna</u> <u><u>had</u></u> good <u>manners</u>.
2. <u>Lewis</u> and <u>Will</u> <u><u>bought</u></u> a new <u>computer</u>.
3. The <u>mailman</u> <u><u>left</u></u> a <u>letter</u> on the <u>doorstep</u> of our <u>house</u>.
4. <u>Jim</u> <u><u>hiked</u></u>, <u><u>swam</u></u>, and <u><u>rode</u></u> his <u>bike</u> during the <u>vacation</u>.
5. <u>Evi</u> and <u>Jacob</u> <u><u>saved</u></u> their <u>money</u> for the <u>ice cream</u>.
6. <u>Sam</u> <u><u>rode</u></u> his new <u>bicycle</u> around the <u>block</u>.
7. We <u><u>noticed</u></u> a <u>mouse</u> in the <u>corner</u> of the <u>room</u>.
8. The <u>fly</u> <u><u>came</u></u> in through the open <u>door</u>, <u><u>flew</u></u> into my <u>lemonade</u> and <u><u>drowned</u></u>.
9. <u>Mary</u> <u><u>recovered</u></u> from her <u>jealousy</u>, <u>anger</u> and <u>unhappiness</u>.
10. <u>Christian</u> and <u>Ethan</u> <u><u>dragged</u></u> their broken <u>bicycles</u> across the <u>street</u>.

Grammar and Punctuation 3
Linking Verbs

Verbs that link words together are called **linking verbs**. The most common linking verbs are forms of the verb *be*:

Forms of the Verb *Be*

am, is, are, was, were, be, been, being

Linking verbs link subjects to nouns, pronouns (words that take the place of nouns), and adjectives (describing words). The noun or adjective after the linking verb describes or renames the subject.

Examples of Linking Verbs

George and *Susan* were very *kind*.

Bob is your *friend*.

Your *brother* was the *president* of the club.

Notice that in the first sentence above, the subjects *George* and *Susan* are linked to the adjective *kind* by the linking verb *were*. In the second sentence, *Bob* is being linked by the verb *is* to the noun *friend*. In the third sentence, the subject *brother* is being linked by the linking verb *was* to the noun *president*.

Exercise 3.1

Memorize the linking verbs.

Exercise 3.2

Underline the linking verbs in the sentences below twice. Underline the nouns that the linking verbs join together once. If the sentence is a question, rewrite the sentence as a statement. The first one has been done for you.

1. Are Christian and Emma siblings?
   Christian and Emma are siblings.

LINKING VERBS

2. Tim and Bill were good students.

3. Jonam is a blond-haired boy.

4. The librarian was a pleasant woman.

5. Our father is the pastor of the church.

6. The papers on the desk are worksheets.

7. Are the boys his sons?   The boys are his sons.

8. Is Elsa Pearl a first-grade student?   Elsa Pearl is a first-grade student.

9. My cousin's name is Charles.

10. Is Mrs. Wilson a good cook?   Mrs. Wilson is a good cook.

Exercise 3.3

Underline the nouns in the following sentences once and the action and linking verbs twice. Again, if the sentence is a question, rewrite the sentence as a statement. The first two have been done for you.

1. Fred was an artist.

2. The king ruled for seven years.

3. His mother planted seeds in her garden and watered the ground.

4. I am not a child anymore.

5. Alexi and his brother bought five pens and five pencils at the store.

6. He sleeps late on Saturdays.

7. Is Tom a student at a local private school?
   Tom is a student at a local private school.

8. He caught a large crab at the shore.

9. Susan counted the days before her birthday.

10. Thomas Lee swims in the summer, but in the winter, he plays indoor tennis.

Grammar and Punctuation 4
The Simple Subject and Verb

Every predicate has a verb and every complete subject has a simple subject, or subject. You have already learned that a verb is a word that shows action or that links two or more words together. The subject of a sentence is the noun that controls the verb. Let's look at the following as examples:

> Tom's mother has baked some oatmeal cookies this afternoon.
>
> The author of *Gulliver's Travels* was an Irish Anglican priest.

The complete predicate of the first sentence is *baked some oatmeal cookies this afternoon.* The verb in the predicate is *has baked.* Notice that that the verb of the sentence includes both the helping verb and the main verb. The complete subject of this sentence contains two words: *Tom's* and mother. To find the subject, or the noun that controls the verb, we ask the question, "Who or what has baked?" The answer is not *Tom's.* It is *mother. Mother*, then, is the subject of the verb *baked,* for it was the mother, not Tom, who baked the cookies.

The predicate in the second sentence contains five words: *was an Irish Anglican priest.* The linking verb of this predicate is *was.* The complete subject also contains five words: *the author of Gulliver's Travels.* To find the subject, we ask the question, "Who or what was an Irish Anglican priest?" The answer to this question is *author.*

THE SIMPLE SUBJECT AND VERB

Exercise 4.1

Underline the complete predicate twice and the complete subject once. Circle the simple subject and the verb, including helping verbs. If the sentence is a question, rewrite it as a statement.

Example 1: My (sister) (is wearing) a green sweater.

Example 2: Have you seen the hot air balloon?
(You) (have seen) the hot air balloon.

1. The (teacher) (put) a happy face sticker on the pupil's page.
2. The (pastor) (was reading) from the New Testament.
3. Is the kite flying very high? The (kite) (is flying) very high.
4. The (leaves) of the oak (were turning) red and yellow.
5. Harry's older (brother) (read) us a story about a pirate.
6. The (winner) of the race (was wearing) a blue ribbon.
7. Does your father listen to Schubert? Your (father) (does listen) to Schubert.
8. The red brick (building) (was being used) as a gymnasium.
9. (We) (had seen) a bear on the camping trip.
10. Was he introduced to your friend? (He) (was introduced) to your friend.

Grammar and Punctuation 5
Helping Verbs and Main Verbs

Can you identify underlined word in the following sentence? Is it an action or linking verb, or something else?

> Jennifer will eat some of your candy.

The word *will* in this sentence is not a linking verb or an action verb. It is a **helping verb**.

Although it has no meaning in itself, a helping verb "helps" the main verb. The helping verb always comes *before* the main verb. If it is an action verb, it is the word that holds the meaning. Together, the main verb and the helping verb form the complete verb. The main verb may be either an action verb or a linking verb, as in the following sentence.

> John is being very helpful today.

The complete verb is *is being*. The main verb *being* is a linking verb; the helping verb is *is*.

One way that helping verbs "help" the main verb is by giving it *tense*, or time. There are six tenses in English: present, past, future, present perfect, past perfect and future perfect. By adding the verb *will*, the verb *eat* is changed into the future tense. You will notice in the list of helping verbs below that some of the linking verbs you have memorized are also helping verbs.

The Helping Verbs

am, is, are, was, were, be, been, being
has, have, had
may, must, might
do, does, did
can, could; shall, should; will, would

HELPING VERBS AND MAIN VERBS

Exercise 5.1

Memorize the helping verbs.

Exercise 5.2

Write down the complete verb of each sentence. Underline the helping verb or verbs once, if there are any, and the main verb twice. There might be more than one helping verb in the sentence or no helping verb. Rewrite questions as statements. Separate contractions.

Example 1: He can't come.
He can not come.   can come

Example 2: I'm very tired.
I am very tired.   am

(There is no helping verb in this sentence.)

Example 3: Did she understand?
She did understand.   did understand

1. Micah has been playing violin for almost two years.   has been playing

2. We have arrived.   have arrived

3. I'm counting on you.   I am counting on you.   am counting

4. They're sitting on the porch.   They are sitting on the porch.   are sitting

5. Did you hear the good news?   You did hear the good news.   did hear

6. She's been resting in her bedroom.
   She has been resting in her bedroom.   has been resting

7. We don't know the answer.   We do not know the answer.   do know

8. The cows were lowing in the pasture.   were lowing

9. Would you set the table?   You would set the table.   would set

10. The children were polite.   were

Grammar and Punctuation 6
Regular and Irregular Verbs

Did you ever notice that verbs change depending on how they are used in a sentence? When a verb is showing a past action or has the words *has*, *have* or *had* in front of it, it often adds the suffix *-d* or *-ed*. These words are called **regular verbs**. Other verbs do not add a suffix, but change their form. These are called **irregular verbs**.

Examples of Regular Verbs

add	added	(has, have, had) added
dance	danced	(has, have, had) danced
pick	picked	(has, have, had) picked

Examples of Irregular Verbs

bring	brought	(has, have, had) brought
eat	ate	(has, have, had) eaten
fall	fell	(has, have, had) fallen

Example Sentences with *Eat*

I *eat* my lunch at noon every day.
I *will eat* my lunch.
I *ate* my lunch at noon today.
I *did eat* my lunch.
I *have* already *eaten* my lunch.

Below is a table of verb forms that are irregular or commonly mistaken.

Table of Verb Forms

Present	Past	After *has, have, had*
become	became	become
begin	began	begun
bite	bit	bitten

REGULAR AND IRREGULAR VERBS

Present	Past	After *has, have, had*
blow	blew	blown
break	broke	broken
burst	burst	burst
buy	bought	bought
catch	caught	caught
choose	chose	chosen
come	came	come
creep	crept	crept
dig	dug	dug
drag	dragged	dragged
drive	drove	driven
forbid	forbade	forbidden
forget	forgot	forgotten
go	went	gone
hurt	hurt	hurt
lie ("recline")	lay	lain
lay ("put")	laid	laid
raise	raised	raised
rise	rose	risen
ring	rang	rung
run	ran	run
shake	shook	shaken
sing	sang	sung
speak	spoke	spoken
swim	swam	swum
swing	swung	swung
take	took	taken
teach	taught	taught
weave	wove	woven
wind	wound	wound
write	wrote	written

Exercise 6.1

Some of the sentences below use an incorrect verb form. If one of the verbs is incorrect, cross it out and write its correct form on a separate piece of paper. If it is correct, write "C." If you have trouble, you can look at the chart on the previous page. The first one has been done for you.

1. Mr. Thomas has ~~buyed~~ a new carpet for his home office.   bought

2. Cold from playing outside in the snow, our little brother ~~blowed~~ on his hands.

3. Has Christian ~~ran~~ the race yet?   run

4. Anna didn't know who was at the door.   C

5. You should have ~~went~~ with the others to the park.   gone

6. Mr. Harold has ~~teached~~ at that school for three years.   taught

7. I could have ~~swam~~ more quickly, but I had stomach cramps.   swum

8. Elise and Evi ~~winded~~ up their toy and it span around the floor for at least a minute.   wound

9. You should have ~~spoke~~ when you had the chance!   spoken

10. He ~~rose~~ his hand to ask a question.   raised

Grammar and Punctuation 7
Voice

When we say that a person is passive, we mean that he does not do things himself; instead, he waits for things to happen to him. Likewise, in grammar, when we say a verb is in the **passive voice**, the subject is not doing the action of the main verb; rather the action of the verb is directed at the subject. However, when the subject *is* doing the action of the verb, we say that the verb in the **active voice**. Generally speaking, it is better to use active voice verb when writing.

Sentence with Active Voice Verb

The man in the yellow cab shouted to his friend on the street.

(Notice that the subject *man* is doing the action of the main verb *shouted*.)

Sentence with Passive Voice Verb

The delicious strawberries had already been eaten by the children.

(Notice that the subject *strawberries* is not doing the action of the main verb *eaten*—strawberries cannot eat! Rather, the children ate the strawberries.)

Exercise 7.1

Underline the subject once and the main verb twice. Then tell whether it is doing the action of the main verb: if it is, write "active"; if not, write "passive." The first one has been done for you.

1. All of the picnic food had been prepared.   passive
2. Edward found his glasses under the sofa.   active
3. Will William be praised for his work?   passive
4. Sarah will understand the problem.   active
5. Some of the pie was eaten.   passive

6. Of the many players, Tommy was picked by the team.   passive

7. We stirred the soup in a large pot.   active

8. Have you been taught manners?   passive

9. Daniel escaped right before their arrival.   active

10. The chickens have been fed.   passive

Exercise 7.2

Rewrite the following sentences so that the verbs are in active voice. Some verbs are in the present tense, while others are in the past tense. Make sure that you change only the *voice* of the verb, not the *tense*. The first one has been done for you.

1. Robert was praised by the coach for his playing.
   The coach praised Robert for his playing.

2. The pretty yellow butterfly was caught by Susan.
   Susan caught the pretty yellow butterfly.

3. Thomas is instructed by wonderful teachers.
   Wonderful teachers instruct (are instructing) Thomas.

4. Anna and her sister Patty are given responsibilities by her.
   She gives Anna and her sister Patty responsibilities.

5. A song was sung by the choir.   The choir sang a song.

6. No words were spoken by the little boy.   The little boy spoke no words.

7. The stick is shaken at the boys by the grumpy old man.
   The grumpy old man is shaking a stick at the boy.

8. Which road was chosen by them?   Which road did they choose?

9. When was the race begun by the runners?
   When did the runners begin the race?

10. A computer was bought by the family every five years.
    The family bought a computer every five years.

Grammar and Punctuation 8
Subjunctive Mood

Did you ever imagine that you were something that you were not—an astronaut or President of the United States? If you have, you are creating a **hypothetical situation**. A hypothetical situation is one that we imagine to be true, but is not. The **subjunctive mood** is used for wishes and hypothetical situations using "if." There are a two things to keep in mind regarding the subjunctive mood: (1) Use a past verb for a present action, and use the helping verb *had* for a past action. (2) Never use *was*; always use *were*.

Not all "if" statements are subjunctive. One can use "if" without creating a hypothetical situation or saying something that is not true. Suppose you say something like "If I have an avocado in the refrigerator, I will eat one." This sentence means that you might or might not eat an avocado, depending on whether or not there is one in the refrigerator. This kind of "if" statement is called a **conditional** statement. By using the subjunctive mood, you are stressing that there in fact aren't any avocados in the refrigerator: *If I had an avocado in the refrigerator, I would eat one.*

Subjunctive Mood

Present action	I wish I **were** (not *was* or *am*) at the park.
Past action	I wish I **had slept** (not *slept*) well last night.
Hypothetical present	If I **studied** (not *study*) hard, I would do better.

To state a mere fact, however, we use the **indicative mood**.

Indicative Mood

Present action	I **am** at the park.
Past action	I **slept** well last night.
Conditional present	If I **study** hard, I do well.

Exercise 8.1

If the sentence using *if* is conditional, write "C"; if it is hypothetical, write "H." Remember that a hypothetical situation is not true. The first one has been done for you.

1. If I were a hippopotamus, I would beware of hunters.   H
2. If I were home, I would be eating now; however, I have to stay at the library for a few more hours.   H
3. If you had told me, this would not have happened!   H
4. If you practice your instrument more, you will get a lot better.   C
5. If I were home, my mother would be preparing better meals.   H

Exercise 8.2

Write a response to the following sentence using a hypothetical "if" clause. Make sure that you use the helping verb *had* for a past action and that you do not use the word *was*. The first two have been done for you.

1. You are not at home.
   If I were at home, I would be cleaning.
2. You were not happy with the car.
   If I had been happy with the car, I would not have complained to the salesperson.
3. You did not see the magician.   If I had seen the magician...
4. You are not with your friend.   If I were with my friend...
5. You are not playing outside.   If I were playing outside...
6. You did not do your homework.   If I had done my homework...
7. You did not swim.   If I had swum...
8. You are not sad.   If I were sad...
9. You are not angry.   If I were angry...
10. You are not in the house.   If I were in the house...

Grammar and Punctuation 9
Nouns and Subject–Verb Agreement

Forming Plurals of Regular Nouns

Nouns can be singular (one) or plural (more than one). Most nouns—but not all—add the letter *s* to become plural. These nouns are called **regular nouns**.

Rules for Plurals of Regular Nouns

- Most regular nouns just add an *s*: *shoe, shoes; pen, pens; garden, gardens*; etc.
- When a regular noun ends in *ch* (as in *church*), *x*, *s*, *ss*, or *sh*, *e* is added before the *s*: *churches, foxes, glasses, dishes*.
- When a noun ends in a consonant and the letter *y* (as in *spy*), the plural is made by changing the *y* to *i* and adding *es*. However, when a noun ends in a vowel and the letter *y* (as in *ray*), the plural is made by just adding an *es*: *spies, rays*.
- Some nouns that end in an *f* sound, such as *wolf, calf* and *knife*, change the *f* to a *v* before adding *s* or *es*: *wolves, calves, knives*.
- When a noun ends in a consonant and the letter *o* (as in *hero*), the plural is usually made by adding *es*. However, when a noun ends in a vowel and the letter *o* (as in *radio*), the plural is made by just adding an *s*: *heroes, radios*. There are exceptions to this rule: some words from Italian or Spanish, such as *piano, solo* and *nacho*, only add an *s* even though these have a consonant before the *o*: *pianos, solos, nachos*.

Exercise 9.1

Memorize the rules regarding making regular nouns plural.

Irregular Nouns

Nouns that have a special form in the plural, or that have a plural that is identical to the singular, are called **irregular nouns**.

Plurals of Some Irregular Nouns

tooth	teeth
woman	women
man	men
mouse	mice
fish	fish (or fishes)
child	children
deer	deer
goose	geese
ox	oxen

Exercise 9.2

Make the following words plural. The first one has been done for you.

1. garage   garages
2. label   labels
3. sky   skies
4. woman   women
5. wax   waxes
6. buoy   buoys
7. search   searches
8. opera   operas
9. tomato   tomatoes
10. viola   violas
11. duo   duos
12. roof   roofs
13. latch   latches
14. ski   skis
15. half   halves

NOUNS AND SUBJECT–VERB AGREEMENT

Exercise 9.3

Make the following words plural. The first one has been done for you.

1. birch   birches
2. box   boxes
3. difficulty   difficulties
4. battle   battles
5. mouse   mice
6. deer   deer
7. stash   stashes
8. cello   cellos
9. loaf   loaves
10. match   matches
11. mosquito   mosquitoes
12. piano   pianos
13. journey   journeys
14. potato   potatoes
15. dress   dress

Subject–Verb Agreement

Verbs must agree with their subjects in number. For example, if a subject is plural, the correct plural form of the verb must be used. When a subject does not agree with its verb, we say that there is a **subject–verb agreement** problem.

Sometimes there is more than one subject in the sentence. In such a case, the subject is plural. When the words *there* and *here* are used, the subject comes *after* the verb.

Bob is my friend.
Bob and Janet are my friends.

There is a box on the floor.
There are a box and a vase on the floor.

Exercise 9.4

Underline the subjects of the following incorrect sentences once and the complete verb (helping verbs and main verbs) twice. Then, rewrite the sentence on a separate piece of paper using the correct verb. If the sentence is a question, rewrite the sentence so that it reads as a statement. If the sentence contains a contraction, rewrite it with the contraction separated. The first two have been done for you.

1. There <u>is</u> a <u>tree</u> and a <u>bush</u> in her garden.
   There are a tree and a bush in her garden.

2. Has your cat and dog been fed yet?
   Your <u>cat</u> and <u>dog</u> <u>has been fed</u> yet.
   Have your cat and dog been fed yet.

3. There <u>is</u> a <u>house</u> and an apartment <u>building</u> on this street.
   There are a house and an apartment building on this street.

4. Has Lewis and Will been mowing the lawn?
   <u>Lewis</u> and <u>Will</u> <u>has been mowing</u> the lawn.
   Have Lewis and Will been mowing the lawn?

5. Only <u>one</u> of the boys <u>are coming</u>.
   Only one of the boys is coming.

6. Has the oxen been taken into the field?
   The <u>oxen</u> <u>has been taken</u> into the field.
   The oxen have been taken into the field.

7. There <u>is</u> a <u>teacher</u> and a <u>parent</u> in that room.
   There are a teacher and a parent in that room.

8. There's some farmers talking in the barn.
   There <u>is</u> some <u>farmers</u> talking in the barn.
   There are some farmers talking in the barn.

9. Here <u>is</u> a <u>pencil</u> and an <u>eraser</u> for you to use.
   Here are a pencil and an eraser for you to use.

10. The <u>car</u> full of children <u>are parked</u> in the driveway.
    The car full of children is parked in the driveway.

Grammar and Punctuation 10
Personal Pronouns (1)

Pronouns are noun substitutes. If we didn't have pronouns, we would be forced to say things like *Mr. Nelson took Mr. Nelson's meal to Mr. Nelson's table to eat before Mr. Nelson left for work.* With pronouns, the sentence sounds much better: *Mr. Nelson took his meal to his table to eat before he left for work.*

The most commonly used kind of pronoun is the **personal pronoun**. There are three **persons** of personal pronouns: first, second and third. The first person is used for the person speaking, the second person is used for the person spoken to, and the third person is used for everyone else. The personal pronouns in the following chart are called the **subjective case** personal pronouns because they are used for subjects.

Subjective Case Personal Pronouns

	Singular	Plural
First person	I	we
Second person	you	you
Third person	he, she, it	they

Exercise 10.1

Memorize the chart of subjective case personal pronouns.

Exercise 10.2

Rewrite the sentences below using *one* subjective case personal pronoun for the underlined subjects.

1. You and Bob should come with me today.   he

2. You and I can have some lemonade when we are finished painting the fence.   We

3. Have Lewis and Jacob thought about what you wanted for your birthday?   they

4. Ethan and <u>Anna</u> have borrowed an interesting new book at the library.   she

5. <u>The dog</u> was rummaging through our trash.   It

Exercise 10.3

Answer questions 1–4 using the following sentence: *The tall man and his wife were ignoring the helpful park ranger's orders regarding their dogs.*

1. The word *were* is ____.
   a) a main verb
   b) a linking verb
   ⓒ) a helping verb
   d) a regular verb
   e) an action verb

2. The word *ignoring* is ____.
   a) a noun
   b) an irregular verb
   c) a passive verb
   ⓓ) a main verb
   e) pronoun

3. Which of the following words is NOT used as a noun in the sentence?
   a) man
   b) woman
   ⓒ) tall
   d) orders
   e) dogs

PERSONAL PRONOUNS (1)

4. Which of the following is NOT true of the sentence?
   a) The sentence is a fragment.
   b) The simple subjects of the sentence are *man* and *wife*.
   c) The sentence has a compound subject.
   d) The complete predicate of the sentence is *were ignoring the helpful park ranger's orders regarding their dogs*.
   e) The complete subject of the sentence is *the tall man and his wife*.

5. Which of the following sentences does NOT have a helping verb?
   a) Harry and I were looking for you.
   b) Thomas and James have helped us.
   c) Do you wear glasses?
   d) Sam's kitten is little.
   e) Will he be coming with us?

Answer questions 6–7 using the following sentence: *If your brother were helped more, he would not get so frustrated.*

6. Which of the following is NOT true about the sentence?
   a) It is written with the subjunctive mood.
   b) The words *were helped* and *would get* express present time.
   c) It is assumed that the speaker does not think that the brother of the person he is talking to is being helped enough.
   d) The word *would* is a main verb.
   e) The word *helped* is a regular verb.

7. Which of the following correctly changes the sentence into *active voice*, without changing other parts of the sentence?
   a) If your brother were being helped more, he would not get so frustrated.
   b) If you were being helped by your brother, he would not get so frustrated.

c) If you had been helping your brother, he would not have been getting so frustrated.
d) If your brother was being helped more, he would not be getting so frustrated.
(e) If you helped your brother more, he would not get so frustrated.

8. Which of the following sentences has a problem with subject-verb agreement?
   a) Will and his brother will be going to a yo-yo contest in town.
   b) There on the swing are John and his sister.
   c) The house full of children is noisy.
   d) Here are your notes on Henry Wadsworth Longfellow.
   (e) Has Anna and Steven learned their grammar lesson?

9. Which of the following is NOT a personal pronoun?
   a) I
   b) you
   (c) this
   d) we
   e) they

10. Which of the following sentences has a mistake in pronoun usage?
    a) You and she are invited.
    b) You and I will sit next to John and him.
    c) The president of the college had tea with his secretary and him.
    (d) Fred, Tom, you and me are good friends.
    e) You and they will have to make a deal.

Grammar and Punctuation 11
Personal Pronouns (2)

You learned in the last lesson that subjective case pronouns are used for subjects. They are also used for **predicate nominatives**. A predicate nominative is a noun or pronoun that comes after a linking verb and renames the subject. In the sentences below, the predicate nominatives are underlined. Notice that they both follow a linking verb (printed in italics).

Examples of Predicate Nominatives

Sam *is* my brother. (The word *brother* renames the subject *Sam*.)

It *was* he who did it. (The word *he* renames the subject *it*.)

Why is the word *he* used in the second sentence rather than *him*? The reason is that *he* is a predicate nominative, and subjective case personal pronouns are used for predicate nominatives. The word *him* is an objective case personal pronoun. Objective case personal pronouns are used when the pronoun is not a subject or predicate nominative.

Objective Case Personal Pronouns

	Singular	Plural
First person	me	us
Second person	you	you
Third person	him, her, it	them

Exercise 11.1

Memorize the chart of objective case personal pronouns.

Exercise 11.2

Rewrite the following sentences using a subjective case personal pronoun for the underlined subjects and predicate nominatives. The first one has been done for you.

1. It was Sarah who left her sweater on the desk.
   It was she who left her sweater on the desk.

2. Jacob and <u>Ethan</u> will be visiting the Philadelphia Museum next week.   he

3. Did <u>Will and Lewis</u> know what time it was?   they

4. My father and <u>brother</u> are weeding the garden now.   he

5. The first person in line was <u>Elise</u>, not <u>Will</u>.   she

Exercise 11.3

Write "subjective" if the underlined word is a subject or predicate nominative. Write "objective" if the underlined word is not a subject or predicate nominative. Then, rewrite the sentence using a subjective case or objective case pronoun. The first one has been done you.

1. <u>Cherith</u> found a gold necklace under a bush in her backyard.   subjective
   <u>She</u> found a gold necklace under a bush in her backyard.

2. Christian told <u>Emma</u> a funny story.   obj.; her

3. It was <u>Jacob</u> hiding behind the tree.   subj.; he

4. Kevin accidentally hit <u>David</u>.   obj.; him

5. Will and <u>Lewis</u> are eating an egg salad sandwich.   subj.; he

6. Will <u>Anna</u> find her gift?   subj.; she

7. The only person sitting there was <u>Natalie</u>.   subj.; she

8. Why don't you sit between John and <u>Jim</u>?   obj.; him

9. <u>Evi</u> and Elise are sitting in the foyer.   subj.; She

10. Did Cherith know <u>Sarah</u>?   obj.; her

PERSONAL PRONOUNS (2)

Exercise 11.4

If the word is a subject or predicate nominative, circle the subjective case pronoun. If the word is not a subject or predicate nominative, circle the objective case pronoun. The first one has been done for you.

1. Tom and ((I), me) will work together during the summer.
2. Was it ((he), him) who was to blame for this?
3. Please put the chair between Robert and (she, (her)).
4. The extravagant gift was for Sam and (we, (us)).
5. The best musicians were Sally and ((she), her).
6. It was ((they), them) who told us the news.
7. John and ((she), her) have similar cars.
8. Give this to Susan and (he, (him)).
9. Did you find (they, (them))?
10. Sarah and ((we), us) boys have bought the food.

Grammar and Punctuation 12
Adjectives

> Boys came to our house.
> Mary's boys came to our house.
> Mary's tall boys came to our house.
> Mary's five tall boys came to our house.
> Those five tall boys came to our house.

In each of the sentences above, a word was added to give more information about the noun *boys*. These words are called **modifiers** because they give us more information about another word or make another word more specific.

There are two kinds of modifiers: adjectives and adverbs. Adjectives are called modifiers because they give more information about nouns and pronouns. Adjectives answer four questions: *How many? What kind? Which one? Whose?* The words *Mary's, tall, five,* and *those* answer the questions *Whose boys? What kind of boys? How many boys?* and *Which boys?* respectively.

Attributive and Predicate Adjectives

Adjectives may come before or after the words that they modify. If they come right before the word that they modify, they are called **attributive adjectives**. Another kind of adjective, the **predicate adjective**, comes after a linking verb (in normal word order) and describes the subject.

Attributive Adjective	He threw the **red, bouncy** ball.
Predicate Adjective	Sam was **angry**.

In the first sentence, the adjectives *red* and *bouncy* are attributive adjectives because they come before the word *ball*, which they both modify. In the second sentence, the adjective *angry* comes after the linking verb *was* and describes the subject *Sam*. It is a predicate adjective.

ADJECTIVES

Exercise 12.1

Memorize the definitions of the following words.

modifier   a word that describes another word, or makes it more specific

adjective   a word that modifies a noun or pronoun

attributive adjective   an adjective that comes before the word it modifies

predicate adjective   an adjective that follows a linking verb and describes the subject

Exercise 12.2

Memorize the questions that adjectives answer.

Exercise 12.3

Identify the underlined adjectives as attributive or predicate. If the sentence is a question, rewrite it as a statement.

Example 1:   Thomas borrowed John's ridiculous book.
attributive

Example 2:   Is laughter contagious?
Laughter is contagious.   predicate

1. Bob wrote a serious story.   attr.

2. Is there a quick solution to the problem?   attr.

3. Her blue eyes sparkled.   attr.

4. Wasn't that a delicious dinner?
   That was not a delicious dinner.   attributive

5. Her plaid dress was ripped by the thorn bush.   attr.

6. The construction workers were very <u>busy</u> yesterday finishing the house.   pred.

7. Mark has been very <u>friendly</u> to our family.   pred.

8. We launched the toy rocket on the <u>bare</u> field.   attr.

9. Are those honey candies very <u>sweet</u>?   pred.

10. The few <u>lone</u> cows in the pasture were lowing.   attr.

Exercise 12.4

Write two adjectives to modify the subjects of each of the following sentences. Underline the adjectives and tell what question they answer.

Example 1: Dogs wagged their tails.
<u>Tom's</u> <u>hungry</u> dogs wagged their tails.   Whose? What kind?

Example 2: Girls and boys lined up to see the juggler.
<u>Twenty</u> <u>excited</u> girls and boys lined up to see the juggler.   How many? What kind?

1. Letters are on the table.

2. Lima beans dropped out of the bag.

3. Jam and jelly were set on the kitchen counter.

4. Children were reading books in the library.

5. Days have gone by.

Grammar and Punctuation 13
Adverbs

Adverbs are modifiers that give us more information about verbs, adjectives and other adverbs. Adverbs answer four questions: *How? When? Where?* and *In what manner?* In the following sentence, each of the underlined words is an adverb.

> Bob walked <u>home</u> <u>very</u> <u>fast</u> <u>today</u>.

In the above sentence, *home* tells us **where** Bob walked; *very* tells us **how** fast he walked; *fast* tells us **the manner** in which he walked; and *today* tells **when** he walked.

Most adjectives can be made into adverbs by adding the suffix *-ly*. The adjectives *patient, happy, simple,* and *polite* become adverbs with the suffix *-ly*: *patiently, happily, simply,* and *politely*. Although most adverbs end in *-ly*, there are many that do not, such as *rather, very, fast,* and *often*. Also, not all words that end in *-ly* are adverbs: the words *friendly, manly,* and *brotherly* all act as adjectives.

Exercise 13.1

Memorize the questions that adverbs answer.

Exercise 13.2

Put one of the adverbs from the word bank before or after the given verb, adjective or adverb to modify it. Underline the adverb and tell what question the adverb answers. Do not use the same adverb more than once.

> Example 1: studied
> studied <u>yesterday</u>   When?
>
> Example 2: lazy
> <u>very</u> lazy   How?

Word Bank: today, home, extremely, loudly, roughly, very, quickly, frequently, sometimes, rather

1. slowly
2. happy
3. travelled
4. wipe
5. cleaned
6. is singing
7. have played
8. carried
9. swiftly
10. sick

today (When?)
home (Where?)
extremely (How?)
loudly (In what manner?)
roughly (In what manner?)
very (How?)
quickly (In what manner?)
frequently (When? How often?)
sometimes (When? How often?)
rather (How?)

Grammar and Punctuation 14
Pronoun Agreement

In a previous lesson we learned that pronouns replace or refer to nouns. When writing, we must be careful to use plural pronouns to replace plural nouns, and singular pronouns to replace singular nouns. When our pronouns do not match up with the words that they replace, we say that there is a **pronoun agreement problem**.

Pronoun Agreement Problem

Incorrect   Some **musician** left ~~their~~ instrument on this chair.

Correct   Some **musician** left **his** instrument on this chair.

The pronoun *their* does not agree with the noun *musician*, as *their* is plural and *musician* is singular. This pronoun agreement problem can be corrected by using the singular pronoun *his* instead.

Pronoun agreement problems often arise when using singular indefinite pronouns, which are listed below.

Singular Indefinite Pronouns

each, either, neither, one
anyone, anybody, anything
someone, somebody, something
no one, nobody, nothing
everyone, everybody, everything

The above pronouns are *always* singular and singular pronouns must be used to refer to them. In the following sentence, *his*, not *their*, is the correct pronoun to use to refer to *everyone*.

Pronoun Agreement with Indefinite Pronouns

Incorrect   It seems **everyone** wanted to have ~~their~~ car washed today.

Correct   It seems **everyone** wanted to have **his** car washed today.

See page 21 to read about subject–verb agreement.

Indefinite pronouns also cause subject–verb agreement problems. It is important to match up the singular indefinite pronouns with singular verbs.

Subject–Verb Agreement with Indefinite Pronouns

Incorrect   **Each** of our guests ~~are~~ welcome to take ~~their~~ seat in the living room.

Correct   **Each** of our guests **is** welcome to take **his** seat in the living room.

In the above sentence, both the singular verb *is* (not *are*) and the singular pronoun *his* (not *their*) agree with the subject *each*.

Exercise 14.1

Underline the correct pronoun in the following sentences.

1. The bank closed (**its**, their) doors last Monday because it was a holiday.
2. Someone left (**his**, their) gloves on the table.
3. Sam wished that the school would not ask (**its**, their) students to wear ties.
4. One of the girls (**is**, are) going to come.
5. Did the computer company hire new employees when (**its**, their) profits went up?
6. Everyone working at the farm did (**his**, their) share of the work.
7. The post office fired one of (**its**, their) employees because the work was slow.
8. The scientific team lost one of (**its**, their) members.
9. Each of the girls recited (**her**, their) poem very well.
10. Only one of the men in the book club will be taking (**his**, their) wife to the conference.

Grammar and Punctuation 15
Prepositions

Below is a list of some common prepositions.

List of Common Prepositions

about, above, across, after, around, aside, at, away, before, below, beside, between, down, during, for, from, in, into, inside, next to, of, on, onto, outside, over, through, to, under, underneath, up, with

Prepositions can do several things in a sentence. One is that they can act as adverbs in a sentence by answering the question "Where?"

Example of Preposition Used as Adverb

The fourth-graders went **away**.

The preposition *away* in the above sentence is an adverb. It modifies the verb *went*, giving us more information about *where* the fourth-graders went.

Exercise 15.1

In each of the following sentences, underline the prepositions once and the verb that it is modifying twice. The first one has been done for you.

1. John quickly <u>ran</u> <u>out</u>.

    (The preposition *out* tells us where he *ran*.)

2. Bob <u>played</u> <u>outside</u> before he left.

3. Bob said, "If you like hayrides, <u>get</u> <u>on</u>!"

4. The balloon escaped his hand and <u>went</u> <u>up</u>.

5. His favorite pet rabbit <u>hopped</u> <u>away</u>.

Grammar and Punctuation 16
Prepositional Phrases

In addition to working as adverbs, prepositions can function in a group of words, called a phrase, to show direction, position, and time. A phrase may be compared to an army, and words to soldiers in the army. One soldier may work in the battlefield. Another may work as a spy. Another may work in the soup kitchen preparing food. But they all work together for one common purpose and that is to win against the enemy. Likewise, a phrase is a group of words, each of which has its individual work to do. But all the words work together for a common purpose.

A prepositional phrase includes at least two words, but may include more. Each of the words has its duty within the phrase. One works as a preposition, joining the phrase to the sentence. Another works as a noun. Yet another may work as a modifier. But all the words work together as a modifier. A prepositional phrase can modify a noun, in which case it is called an **adjectival prepositional phrase**. It can also modify a verb, in which case it is called an **adverbial prepositional phrase**.

Example of an Adjectival Prepositional Phrase

The book on the dirty table belongs to my brother.

The prepositional phrase *on the dirty table* tells us the position of the book in relation to the table. Because it gives us more information about the noun *book*, the phrase is adjectival.

Example of an Adverbial Prepositional Phrase

We walked into the beautiful garden.

The words in the prepositional phrase *into the garden* work together to modify the verb *walked*, and therefore the prepositional phrase would be considered adverbial.

You have already learned that modifiers can make a sentence clearer

PREPOSITIONAL PHRASES

and more interesting. Adding descriptive detail to sentences, though, may involve more than single-word adjectives and adverbs. Adjectival and adverbial prepositional phrases are important additions to a sentence to make a sentence more colorful, clear, and specific.

Exercise 16.1

Memorize the definitions of the following words.

> **preposition**   a part of speech that shows, among other things, direction, position, and time
>
> **phrase**   a group of words that work together as one
>
> **prepositional phrase**   a phrase that has a preposition, a noun, and any modifiers
>
> **adjectival prepositional phrase**   a prepositional phrase that modifies a noun or pronoun
>
> **adverbial prepositional phrase**   a prepositional phrase that modifies a verb, adjective or adverb

Exercise 16.2

Add an adjectival prepositional phrase after each of the subjects in the following sentences. Circle the subject and underline the adjectival prepositional phrase. Use only prepositions from the word bank.

> Example: The gift was a secret.
> The (gift) from Elizabeth's mother was a secret.
>
> Word Bank: inside, before, of, after, next to, under, on top of

1. The (puppy) belongs to Miriam.
2. The (village) was burned.
3. The (books) fell into my lap.
4. The (parents) scolded us.
5. The (intermission) was fifteen minutes long.

Exercise 16.3

Add adverbial prepositional phrases to the following sentences to add information about the verb, telling how, when, where or in what manner the action was done. Circle the verb and underline the adverbial prepositional phrases. Use prepositions only from the word bank.

Example: Harry made his decision.
Harry (made) his decision <u>after three days</u>.

Word Bank: on, around, after, in, before, by, at

1. The actors greeted us.
2. The student read the poem.
3. Did she wash the windows?
4. Paul invited our brothers.
5. Last year we travelled.

on (Where?)
around (Where?)
after (When?)
in (Where?)
before (When?)
by (In what manner? Where?)
at (Where? When?)

Grammar and Punctuation 17
Coordinating Conjunctions

Conjunctions are words that connect. They may join single words, groups of words, or even whole sentences together. There are several different kinds of conjunctions, but we will be going over just one kind right now. It is called the **coordinating conjunction**. Because there are not many coordinating conjunctions, they will be easy to memorize. The most common ones are listed below.

List of Coordinating Conjunctions

and, but, or, nor

These words are useful in connecting subjects and verbs. When they connect subjects, the combined set of words is called a compound subject. When they connect verbs, the combined set of verbs is called a compound verb.

Separate Subjects	David might go. Lydia might go.
Compound Subjects	David or Lydia might go.
Separate Verbs	Samuel sleds. Samuel skates.
Compound Verbs	Samuel sleds and skates.

Short unconnected sentences often sound choppy and clipped. When sentences are joined with coordinating conjunctions, the sentence group is more elegant.

Short Clipped Sentences

I walked to my friend's house. I knocked on the door. Mrs. Black answered. I asked if David could come out to play. She said that David was not at home.

Sentences Joined with Coordinating Conjunctions

I walked to my friend's house and knocked at the door. Mrs. Black answered. I asked if David could come out to play, but she said that he was not at home.

Notice that a comma comes before the word *and* and *but* when these words join sentences. The coordinating conjunction *and* or *but* can often be replaced by a punctuation mark called a semicolon (;). A semicolon joins two sentences that are alike. By using a semicolon, the writer suggests a connection between the two sentences. Look at the following pairs of sentences:

Mary played and I slept.
Mary played; I slept.

Bob thought that the choir sang beautifully, but I didn't.
Bob thought that the choir sang beautifully; I didn't.

Exercise 17.1

Memorize all four conjunctions listed.

Exercise 17.2

Join the following sentences using either a coordinating conjunction or a semicolon. Do not use a semicolon if the sentences are not in some way related. When joining sentences, you may have to get rid of a word or two.

Example 1: Tom took a tissue from the box on the table. He blew his nose.
Tom took a tissue from the box on the table and blew his nose.

Example 2:
I explained to Jim why I could not go. He did not understand.
I explained to Jim why I could not go; he did not understand.
I explained to Jim why I could not go, but he did not understand.

COORDINATING CONJUNCTIONS

1. Alysia and David took their books. They read a story called *Three Months Under the Snow.*
   Alysia and David took their books and read a story called *Three Months Under the Snow.*

2. Tom and Rachel are my friends. They have always been my friends, ever since I can remember.
   Tom and Rachel are my friends and have been ever since I can remember.

3. I like swimming. Bob likes playing tennis.
   I like swimming; Bob likes playing tennis.
   I like swimming, but Bob likes playing tennis.

4. My mother called us inside for dinner. We took our places at the table.
   My mother called us inside for dinner, and we took our places at the table.

5. Alice ran down the sidewalk. She tripped over a little rock in her way. She was not hurt.
   Alice ran down the sidewalk; she tripped over a little rock in her way, but she was not hurt.

Exercise 17.3

The sentences in the following paragraph are short and choppy. Join them using conjunctions.

Today we went to gym. We did gymnastics. We did somersaults. There was one girl who could not do them as well. I asked her why. She replied, "I don't think I'm flexible enough." I got a warning for talking with her. After our class, we packed up. We went back to math class.

Grammar and Punctuation 18
Subordinating Conjunctions

Up to this point you have learned about *coordinating* conjunctions. The word *coordinating* comes from the prefix *co-* which means "together" and the root *ordinate*, which means "to put in order." These conjunctions join sentences together equally; that means that both sentences are equal in importance and are independent, or can stand alone.

There is another kind of conjunction called the **subordinating conjunction**. The prefix of this word is *sub-*, which means "under." Unlike coordinating conjunctions, which makes two sentences equal, subordinating conjunctions puts one part of the sentence "under" another. In other words, it makes it dependent.

Sentence Joined by Coordinating Conjunction

Ray and Susan travelled to Nevada, **but** Charles stayed home.

Notice that both parts of the sentence are equal in importance. The one is not dependent on the other.

Sentence Joined by Subordinating Conjunctions

Elizabeth cried **because** her big brother took away her doll.

Here, the subordinating conjunction *because* makes the second underlined part dependent. It cannot stand alone. The subordinating conjunction also shows a relationship between the two parts. Do you see what that relationship is? It is a *cause and effect* relationship. The second part of the sentence has caused the first part of the sentence.

Her big brother took away her doll ⟶ Elizabeth cried.

There are other relationships that subordinating conjunctions show, like a relationship in time, as in the following sentence:

Tom hummed while he worked.

SUBORDINATING CONJUNCTIONS

The subordinating conjunction *while* shows a relationship in time; it shows that the subject *Tom* hummed at the same time he worked.

Let us summarize the things you ought to know, then, about subordinating conjunctions:

- They join sentences together.

- They make one part dependent on another part.

- They show a relationship.

Some of the more common subordinating conjunctions include the following:

List of Common Subordinating Conjunctions

after, although, as, as if, because, before, if, since, though, until, when, where, while

Exercise 18.1

Memorize the listed subordinating conjunctions.

Exercise 18.2

Underline the subordinating conjunctions in the following sentences.

Example: <u>When</u> Alycia raised her hand, another student blurted out the answer.

1. <u>Although</u> Terry was frightened, she went inside and faced her aunt.
2. I will not be traveling to Nevada <u>since</u> our relatives will be visiting us in the spring.
3. Bob talked <u>while</u> everyone listened.
4. <u>After</u> we ate dinner, the adults went into the living room to talk.
5. Did they finish the project <u>before</u> you did?

Exercise 18.3

The following sentences have either coordinating conjunctions or subordinating conjunctions. Underline the conjunctions in the following sentences and label them coordinating or subordinating. The first one has been done for you.

1. <u>If</u> Janet does not pick up the groceries from the supermarket, we will not be able to prepare dinner.
   coordinating

2. <u>Although</u> the weather was pleasant, many people did not come to the picnic.   sub.

3. <u>When</u> we heard the loud noise from outside, many of us panicked.   sub.

4. Zach raked the leaves, <u>and</u> our father burned them on the street.   co.

5. <u>As</u> Bradley went indoors, he heard someone shout his name.   sub.

6. Lydia told Lloyd the secret about the surprise birthday party, <u>but</u> made him promise not tell it to anyone.   co.

7. Samuel sculpted <u>while</u> his brother read.   sub.

8. Harry had not told us the story, <u>nor</u> had his father.   co.

9. We could not stay <u>because</u> we were in a rush.   sub.

10. Gary talks <u>as if</u> he had visited the place.   sub.

SUBORDINATING CONJUNCTIONS

Exercise 18.4

The following sentences are joined by coordinating conjunctions. Cross out the coordinating conjunction and add an appropriate subordinating conjunction. You may have to reword the sentence or put the conjunction in a different place. Do not use a conjunction more than once.

> Example: The woman complained ~~and~~ the man got angry.
> <u>As</u> the woman complained, the man got angry.

1. Bob whistled too loudly and I was annoyed.
2. I did my outdoor chores and my mother cooked dinner.
3. I did not have time, but I finished my homework.
4. The boy spoke harshly to his sister and his sister cried.
5. Austin first ate his dinner and then he ate his mother's brownies.

Grammar and Punctuation 19
Quotations (1)

Quotation marks are put around exactly what someone has said. There are always two sets of marks, which look like this: " " . The first pair of marks shows the beginning of what someone has said, and the second pair shows the end of what someone has said. Look at the following example of quotation marks:

> Benjamin asked his brother's tutor, "How many hours are you staying?"

What did Benjamin ask his brother's tutor? We can find out by looking in between the quotation marks: *How many hours are you staying?* Notice that there is another punctuation mark before the first quotation marks. It is a comma. A comma always comes right before the quotation mark when introduced by the words *said, ask, exclaim, yell, shout, state, reply, retort,* etc. Notice also that the quotation in this example begins with the word *How*, which is capitalized. The first word of every quotation should be capitalized.

Sometimes a writer records what someone has said word for word. If so, he is recording *exactly* what has been said. But sometimes what a writer records is not word for word. Such quotations are called **indirect quotations**, which do not use quotation marks.

> Karen said that she couldn't come.

What did Karen say exactly? We don't know because the sentence contains an indirect quotation. The writer has not recorded word for word what Karen said, but the general idea is that she couldn't come.

QUOTATIONS (1)

Exercise 19.1

Put commas and quotation marks where they are missing in the following sentences. Some sentences do not need quotation marks because the statements are not quoted verbatim; for these sentences, write "NV" for "not verbatim." Remember to capitalize the first word of every quotation.

Example 1: James asked Jim do you want to go to the soccer game today?
James asked Jim, "Do you want to go to the soccer game today?"

Example 2: Billy replied that he didn't want ice cream tonight.
NV

1. Bob said that Christians should not do such things.   NV

2. At the end of the large table, we heard Grandma say in a wee voice, "No one has tried my sausage cakes."

3. Grandma said that she had made the cakes with fresh pig stomach.   NV

4. Fred told his classmates, "The test is difficult and I know you'll have to study hard for it."

5. Little Benjamin asked Mr. Walter how long he was going to stay.   NV

6. Tom asked Harry why had he taken so long.   NV

7. Tom asked Harry, "Why did you take so long?"

8. He asked us, with a twinkle in his eye, "Why did you come so early?"

9. Tom explained what happened by saying, "I think he tried to get inside by using a crowbar."

10. Bob asked where she had gotten the crowbar.   NV

GRAMMAR & PUNCTUATION 19

Exercise 19.2

Follow the directions given for Exercise 19.1.

Example 1: Micah said look what Elsa did! She wrote her name.
Micah said, "Look what Elsa did! She wrote her name."

Example 2: I ran inside to tell my mother that the mail had come. NV

1. The mother was surprised and exclaimed, "Where did you get that?"

2. Too nervous to speak, Fred said that he couldn't tell them why he had come.   NV

3. Bob wondered why he couldn't have gotten there first.   NV

4. After eating his breakfast, the boy declared to his mother, "Mom, that egg hit the spot!"

5. Tom asked everybody where the next meeting was going to be.   NV

6. Joel said that he had more homework to do.   NV

7. John asked permission to go.   NV

8. At noon Mother called out, "Lunch! Come and get it!"

9. From the hole in the ground we heard the plumber say, "Please give me some light down here."

10. He picked up the eraser and said, "Could I borrow this?"

QUOTATIONS (1)

Exercise 19.3

Follow the directions given for Exercise 19.1.

1. The student in the back of the classroom whispered to his neighbor, "I have a frog in my pocket."
2. When he was asked why he never wore his coat, the little boy replied that his mother didn't want him to get it dirty.   NV
3. The little boy queried, "Who was that man, Mommy?"
4. I said that I knew the answer, but as it turned out, I didn't.   NV
5. She opened the box and exclaimed, "Just what I wanted!"
6. When asked about her age, the little girl replied, clutching her doll, "Mommies don't tell their age."
7. Ronald went to the desk and told the librarian what book she was looking for.   NV
8. Rachel went to the desk and told the librarian, "I'm looking for a book about horses; could you please help me?"
9. The wicked Assyrian king declared, "Every man and woman must worship me."
10. Alexander the Great ordered the people to worship him as a god.   NV

Grammar and Punctuation 20
Quotations (2)

Sometimes quotations are not introduced. In these sentences the punctuation is a little different.

> "Mmm, Grandma, these sausage cakes taste delicious,"
> Father said very sincerely.

In this example, the comma is put before the second set of quotation marks. Whenever the words *ask*, *said*, etc. come after the quotation marks, be sure to punctuate the sentence this way.

The punctuation is different when the direct quotation is a question or an exclamation. In these instances, no comma is needed; just put the end quotation marks right after the question mark or exclamation point, as in the following two examples:

> "Are the sausage cakes good?" asked Fiona.
> "What a beautiful day it was!" James exclaimed.

Exercise 20.1

Put commas, question marks and quotation marks where they are missing in the following sentences.

1. "I really liked that lemon tea," Bill said.
2. "And what did you put in it?" his wife inquired.
3. "Lemon, of course," Bill replied.
4. "Mr. Wombley will be coming over for dinner tonight!" exclaimed Alicia's mom.
5. "Who's Gentleman Wombley?" queried Alicia.
6. "He is a grammar handyman who knows how to fix broken sentences and misplaced commas," her mom said.

QUOTATIONS (2)

7. "Brian made a picture of a rabbit today in Kindergarten class," said Alicia.

8. "It looks more like a bat—but don't tell him that," she added.

9. "It looks like snow outside today," Brian said.

10. "I don't think so," snapped Sally, who didn't like snow at all.

Exercise 20.2

Put quotation marks, commas, and capital letters where needed in the following sentences. Some of the sentences begin with quotations, some end with a quotation, and others have no quotations at all.

1. "The argument started when he came into the room," John said.

2. "It did not!" Bob said.

3. Caitlyn asked, "Why did France sell all that land to America?"

4. "Because it badly needed money," explained her teacher.

5. "But why did it need money?" he asked.

6. The teacher replied, "Because its king Napoleon was leading wars against many nations."

7. George thought that he had left his lunch at home.   (correct)

8. George thought, "Did I leave my lunch at home?"

9. Harry asked what time it was.   (correct)

10. Harry asked, "What time is it?"

Exercise 20.3

Put the commas and quotation marks where needed. Some of the sentences below begin with a quotation; others do not. Some sentences do not need any quotation marks. Capitalize if necessary.

1. My grandfather told me, "I never did like those sausage cakes, but I was afraid to tell Grandma and hurt her feelings."
2. "Why not?" my younger brother queried.
3. Rachel asked Benjamin, "What are you doing on the windowsill?"
4. John looked at his sister and said, "Is that my sweater you're wearing?"
5. Karen joked to her starving husband that she forgot to make dinner.   (correct)
6. "John said that I need a license to drive this," said little Benjamin, pointing to his tricycle.
7. "He was just teasing you," his older sister said.
8. Fred said that he wanted more juice.   (correct)
9. Becky looked into the refrigerator and shouted up the stairwell, "Who drank all the apple juice?"
10. "What a beautiful day it was today!" the little old lady declared.

Grammar and Punctuation 21
Quotations (3)

Sometimes a writer will interrupt a quotation. Notice how the sentence is punctuated when this is done.

> "Becky, when John gets home," her mother said, "tell him that Mrs. Balini called and that she didn't get a paper."

What's different about this sentence and the ones we learned previously? You will first notice there is an additional comma. There is not only one after the first part of the sentence but also one right before the second part of the sentence. Notice what is capitalized: only the beginning of the first part of the quotation, not the beginning of the second part. Also notice that *her* is not capitalized.

Let's review the three kinds of sentences we have gone over so far:

Quotation Introduced

Harry said, "It's raining outside."

Quotation Without Introduction

"It's raining outside," Harry said.

Quotation Interrupted

"If it's raining outside," Harry said, "I'd better get my umbrella."

Exercise 21.1

Put quotation marks and commas where needed. Also capitalize when necessary.

1. "If that's what he wants," declared John, "that's what he'll get."
2. "When Fred gets up," Mother said, "tell him that Grandma's sausage cakes are waiting for him at the breakfast table."
3. "After the test was over," said the student, "I wiped my brow with relief."
4. "Even before I started the test," Bob said, "I knew I wouldn't do well."

5. "Unless you improve your attitude," the teacher said to the disobedient pupil, "you won't do well in your work."

6. "Before I met him," Tom said, "I thought he was always serious."

7. "I want to know," Father said firmly, "who left these roller skates in the driveway."

8. "In less than five minutes," the newspaper article stated, "the race car had traveled 25 miles."

9. "Father," little Billy Boskie asked, "why do cats have whiskers?"

10. "During the 1800s," the professor said, "American sailors would often leave for years at a time."

Exercise 21.2

Correct the sentences below that are improperly punctuated and capitalized.

1. "Where is my calligraphy pen?," queried Katie.   (remove comma)

2. Scott said to her, "I'm using it. But if you aren't nice to me, I won't give it back."

3. "What's in Mr. Walter's bag?" they asked.

4. "We want to see what you are hiding", David said.

5. "My Dad went to Australia," Thomas said.

6. Francis said, "Because the Six Nations had sold the land to English, the territory belonged to them not the French."

7. Reginald said, "that the boys enjoy swimming," but I don't think they do.   (remove comma and quotation marks)

8. "I want to give a speech on soldiers, too," Sam said.

9. Thomas asked, "Did you go to the Shady Maple in Lancaster County?"

10. "Even though Scott likes to draw pictures of airplanes," his sister said, "he would really prefer to fly them."

Grammar and Punctuation 22
Commas (1)

Generally speaking, a comma is used where there would be a pause in speech. It is also used to avoid confusion in a sentence. But there are more specific rules that will help you use commas correctly.

When you address somebody, you often pause before or after you say their name. To indicate that pause in a sentence, you use a comma, as in the sentence "John, will come here for a moment?" The word *John* is called a **noun of direct address**. Always put a comma before, after, or before and after a noun of direct address in the sentence, depending on where it appears in the sentence.

Examples of Nouns of Direct Address

Sam, please give this to Susan.
Hello, Lisa!
The pencils, Karen, are in the drawer.

Commas also should be used after words such as *yes* and *no*, as well as after interjections such as *wow, ouch, whew, whoa,* and *ha*.

Commas After *Yes, No,* and Interjections

Whew, I was glad to get into the air conditioning!
Yes, I understand.

Exercise 22.1

Place a comma in the sentence where it is needed.

1. Do you know the answer to this math problem, David?

2. I don't know, Billy, where you left your coat.

3. Francis, please take out the trash.

4. No, I don't think it matters where Anna places the gift.

5. Wow, that was a long day!

6. Yes, Billy, I think you should apologize to your sister.

7. What are you doing with your mother's watering can, Thomas?

8. Lewis, do you know where your sister is?

9. No, I don't think he will come to the concert if he wasn't invited.

10. Yes, I did ask Thomas if he could do that for me.

Exercise 22.2

Answer questions 1–4 using the following sentence: *When I peeked out the window yesterday at 7:00 this morning, I saw Tom's athletic brother and his friend running in his bare feet across the large field next to my house.*

1. Which of the following in the sentence is not used as a preposition?
    a) at
    b) in
    (c) his
    d) across
    e) next to

2. Which of the following words is used as an adverb in the sentence?
    (a) yesterday
    b) Tom's
    c) feet
    d) field
    e) the

3. Which of the following words is not used an adjective in the sentence?
    a) athletic
    b) Tom's
    (c) morning
    d) his
    e) large

COMMAS (1)

4. Which of the following words is as a subordinating conjunction used in the sentence?
   a) I
   b) peeked
   c) and
   (d) when
   e) across

5. Which of the following sentences has a mistake in pronoun agreement?
   a) Someone left his violin in the music room.
   b) The school allowed students to wear their informal clothing on the field trip.
   c) Elise and Emma told their mother that they were going out to play with the neighbor's dog Zeus.
   (d) The stamp club said that they would be charging higher membership fees next January.
   e) Anybody weeding Mrs. Giegrich's garden will have to buy his own gardening gloves.

6. Which of the following is NOT an objective case pronoun?
   (a) he
   b) her
   c) them
   d) us
   e) me

Write the letter "C" next to the sentence if the punctuation is correct; otherwise, fix the mistake.

7. Tom said to his sister, "Do you see what I see"?

8. "When I came into the room," my friend said, ("She stood up and greeted me."   (no capital)

9. "I found a penny on the sidewalk!" the little girl exclaimed.   C

10. My mother asked me, "Did you take out the trash?"

Grammar and Punctuation 23
Commas (2)

You have learned several uses of the comma so far: with quotation marks, nouns of direct address, and with words such as *yes* and *no* and interjections. Although there are many other rules regarding commas, we will learn just two more. First, a comma is used to separate items in a list, or series, of things. The list may be made up of two or more nouns, verbs, phrases, or clauses. A comma is not necessary before the conjunction unless the sentence would be confusing without it.

Comma Separating Items in a List

I had to go out to get flour, eggs, baking powder and butter.

Thomas pouted, screamed and cried.

Our dog ran into the room, under the dining room table and under the sofa.

The girl petted the rabbit's soft, smooth hair.

I recently bought a rare and expensive book.

Notice that there is no comma in the last sentences, as there are only two items in the list.

Second, commas are used after a long prepositional phrase or subordinate clause. A **subordinate clause** begins with a subordinating conjunction. It contains a subject and verb, but it is not a sentence because it cannot stand alone.

You may review the subordinating conjunctions beginning on page 46.

Comma After Long Phrases or Clauses

In the beginning of our trip to the Adirondack Mountains last summer, my brother lost his tent.

If you come, you will have to bring your own equipment.

When it rains hard, our basement gets flooded.

COMMAS (2)

Exercise 23.1

Place exactly one comma in the sentence where it is possible or needed.

1. If you come late, make sure that you close the door.
2. When I was only sixteen, I traveled through Europe with my father.
3. Although his new watch broke, the store will replace it.
4. Even though his coat was expensive, it started to fray in no time.
5. Sam went into the car, shut the door and turned on the ignition.
6. We admired the child's neat beautiful handwriting.
7. After a party celebrating John's sixteenth birthday last Tuesday, our father took us to see our aunt.
8. He had to take a shower, wash his hair and put on his dress clothes for tonight's concert.
9. Please bring a spiral-bound notebook, paper and a pencil.
10. Before you begin your hike, be sure to drink enough water.

Grammar and Punctuation 24
Apostrophes (1)

Apostrophes are used in two ways. They are used in the place of letters and to show ownership.

Possessive Case

When the letter *s* is added to a noun, the noun is made plural: *tent* becomes *tents*; *lady* becomes *ladies*; and so on.

> Micah's raccoon talks!

The punctuation mark right after the word *Micah* in the above sentence is called an **apostrophe**. It is there to show ownership, for it is *Micah's* raccoon that we are talking about, not anyone else's. The noun, then, does not become plural with the added *s*; instead, the noun becomes *possessive*. A **possessive noun** (a noun with an apostrophe and an *s*) shows that something belongs to or is "of" the person or thing that the noun stands for. Thus:

- *Micah's raccoon* means that the raccoon belongs to Micah.
- *Vanessa's father* means "the father of Vanessa."

Exercise 24.1

Rewrite the underlined portion of the sentence to explain what it means.

> Example 1: <u>Joel's friend</u> is Benjamin.
> the friend of Joel

> Example 2: That is <u>Mother's hat</u>.
> the hat belonging to Mother

1. <u>Mr. Wilson's son</u> is polite.   the son of Mr. Wilson
2. <u>The watch's band</u> is broken.   the band of the watch
3. Who found <u>Uncle Jake's shoes</u>?   the shoes belonging to Uncle Jake

APOSTROPHES (1)

4. Our father likes the neighborhood's parks.   the parks in the neighborhood

5. The children stared at the policeman's gun.
   the gun belonging to the policeman

6. Did Christian's sister bake a lemon cake with her mother?
   the sister of Christian

7. Was Will's book an adventure or mystery book?
   the book belonging to Will

8. I think that Lewis's uncle from Ohio will be visiting on Tuesday.
   the uncle of Lewis

9. I ate a piece of one of Mary's cherry pies last night.
   the cherry pies made by Mary

10. One of Evi's brothers is named Alexi.   the brothers of Evi

Exercise 24.2

Write out the following phrases using an apostrophe. The first one has been done for you.

1. the shoes belonging to the woman
   the woman's shoes

2. the hair of the ox   the ox's hair

3. the oranges belonging to the boy   the boy's oranges

4. the radio belonging to the girl   the girl's radio

5. the computer belonging to Rachel   Rachel's computer

6. the paper belonging to Chris   Chris's paper

7. the house of the dog   the dog's house

8. the dictionary belonging to Leicester   Leicester's dictionary

9. the backyard of John and Chris   John and Chris's backyard

10. the shine of the glass   the glass's shine

Grammar and Punctuation 25
Apostrophes (2)

Personal Pronouns

Many people confuse nouns with pronouns when they use apostrophes. Personal pronouns, unlike nouns, do not add an *s*. Instead, they change form:

> That book belongs to *me*.
> That is *my* book.
>
> That house belongs to *them*.
> That is *their* house.

Many students fall into the trap of using apostrophes where they are not necessary. Possessive personal pronouns already show ownership. The following is a list of these pronouns to keep an eye on so that you don't make a mistake by using an apostrophe with them.

List of Possessive Personal Pronouns

my, mine	our, ours
his	your, yours
her, hers	their, theirs

Exercise 25.1

Correct the following sentences. Some sentences have apostrophes when they should not. Others do not have any when they should. If the sentence is correct, write "C."

1. Is this pencil ~~your's~~ yours?

2. ~~Georges~~ George's life was a hard one.

3. Was it Auntie's birthday yesterday?   C

4. The ~~dogs~~ dog's house was huge and had an air conditioner.

5. ~~It's~~ Its house was huge and had an air conditioner.

Grammar and Punctuation 26
Apostrophes (3)

Regular plural nouns are not made possessive by adding an apostrophe and the letter *s*. They merely add an apostrophe and nothing else. This is the rule for all plural nouns ending in an *s*.

> The boys' hats are on the rack.

Some nouns, however, do not end in *s* in the plural. These nouns are irregular. *Mouse, man, ox, moose, deer, child, tooth,* and *goose* are some examples. The plural forms of these words are *men, oxen, moose, deer, children, teeth,* and *geese*. To make these nouns possessive, you must add an apostrophe and an *s*: *men's suits, oxen's yoke, children's toys*, etc.

See page 22 to review irregular nouns.

Exercise 26.1

Tell whether the underlined word is a possessive noun or not. If the word is a possessive noun, correct the word by adding an apostrophe in the proper place. Do not change the words that are not underlined.

Example 1: librarian's <u>glasses</u>
not possessive

Example 2: little <u>boys</u> lunch box
possessive; boy's

1. The origami <u>papers</u>   not possessive
2. the <u>clocks</u> and watches   not possessive
3. the <u>books'</u> covers   possessive
4. the <u>magician's</u> trick   possessive
5. the red <u>wagons</u>   not possessive
6. <u>cars</u> in the lot   not possessive
7. the four <u>birds'</u> wings   possessive
8. <u>bananas</u> at the grocery store   not possessive

9. table <u>manners</u>   not possessive

10. the round <u>table's</u> three legs   possessive

Exercise 26.2

Write out the following phrases using possessive nouns.

    Example 1: the feathers of the geese
the geese's feathers

    Example 2: the box of candies
the candies' box

1. the shoes of the women   the women's shoes

2. the car of Mr. Reynolds   Mr. Reynolds's car

3. the yoke of the oxen   the oxen's yoke

4. the eraser of the pencil   the pencil's eraser

5. the dessert of the girls   the girls' dessert

Exercise 26.3

Write out the following phrases using possessive nouns.

    Example 1: the books belonging to the two libraries
the two libraries' books

    Example 2: the clean uniforms of the Boy Scouts
the Boy Scouts' clean uniforms

1. the dresses of the ladies   the ladies' dresses

2. the balloon belonging to Benjamin and Micah
Benjamin and Micah's balloon

3. the plants belonging to Mrs. Jones   Mrs. Jones's plants

4. the french fries of the cooks   the cooks' french fries

5. the sons of the parents   the parents' sons

APOSTROPHES (3)

6. the children of the mothers   the mothers' children

7. the leather bag belonging to Mr. Walter
Mr. Walter's leather bag

8. the paws of the dog   the dog's paws

9. the colors of the rainbow   the rainbow's colors

10. the flavors of the candies   the candies' flavors

Exercise 26.4

Write out the following phrases using possessive nouns or pronouns.

Example 1: the kitchen utensils that belong to him
his kitchen utensils

Example 2: the glasses belonging to the women
the women's glasses

1. the house belonging to them   their house

2. the top button of the dress   the dress's top button

3. the weapons of the enemies   the enemies' weapons

4. the tails of the monkeys   the monkeys' tails

5. the teeth of the child   the child's teeth

6. the flowers of my mother-in-law   my mother-in-law's flowers

7. the blades of the knives   the knives' blades

8. the evidence of the lawyers   the lawyers' evidence

9. the signatures of the men   the men's signatures

10. the antlers of the deer   the deer's antlers

Exercise 26.5

Rewrite the following sentences correctly.

Example 1: The dog hurt it's paw.
The dog hurt its paw.

1. Toms mother bought some glove's and mitten's.
   Tom's mother bought some gloves and mittens.

2. Bob and Tim forgot their hat's.
   Bob and Tim forgot their hats.

3. Father gave us these papers, but who gave Karen and Susan their's?
   Father gave us these papers, but who gave Karen and Susan theirs?

4. That ducks feathers were oily.
   That duck's feathers were oily.

5. Mary and Pat were cold, and so we returned the girl's coats.
   Mary and Pat were cold, and so we returned the girls' coats.

Grammar and Punctuation 27
Capitals

You have observed that words beginning a sentence and a quotation are always capitalized, even if the quotation is not a complete sentence. In the example sentences below, the capitalized words are underlined.

Examples of Capitalized Words

"Don't go out in the rain!" my mother said.

The woman behind the stand said, "The string beans are really fresh. My brother John picked them only two hours ago."

His father said, "Exactly!"

Certain nouns are also capitalized. (Remember that a noun is the name of a person, place, thing or idea.) Capitalization rules depend on the language and time period. In German, *all* nouns are capitalized, and in many older works written in English, many nouns are capitalized that are not today. Read the following sentence from the Declaration of Independence:

> We hold these truths to be self-evident, that all men are created equal, that they are endowed by their Creator with certain unalienable Rights, that among these are Life, Liberty, and the pursuit of Happiness.

Can you tell which of the capitalized nouns from this excerpt would be capitalized today?

Today, proper nouns are capitalized, while common nouns are not. Proper nouns are names for specific people, places and things. However, common nouns, as the name suggests, do not name specific nouns. Adjectives formed from proper nouns, called proper adjectives, are also capitalized, such as *German* and *American Indian*. Look at the following examples of common and proper nouns.

Examples of Common Nouns

parent, teacher, child, people, religion

country, state, city, township, area, building

club, league, organization, college, company, law, bill, ordinance

Examples of Proper Nouns

Mr. Wilson, Elizabeth Jacobs, Billy, Puritans, Hindu

Italy, Ohio, Philadelphia, Haverford Township, the West, the Empire State Building

The Havertown Stamp Club, The Broomall Little League, The Wayne Business Association, Haverford College, Standard Oil Company, Newtown Square Curfew Ordinance

Notice that the names in the proper noun column are specific, while the names in the common noun column are not. Also notice that while specific areas (the North, the South) are capitalized, directions (north, south, east, west) are not. Calendar events are capitalized, such as days of the week, months of the year, and holidays; the names of the seasons, however, are not capitalized.

Sentences Containing Proper Nouns

My uncle works at home on <u>Mondays</u> and <u>Tuesdays</u>, but last week, he took the train into <u>Philadelphia</u>.

<u>New Year's Day</u> is a national holiday celebrated near the very beginning of winter.

Were the <u>Pilgrims</u> more like the <u>Huguenots</u> or the <u>Puritans</u>?

Is your anniversary in <u>May</u> or <u>June</u>?

Last spring <u>Harry Nelson</u> went to the <u>Northeast</u> to visit the <u>Craigie House</u>, the old home of <u>Henry Wadsworth Longfellow</u> and then traveled southward to visit the <u>Empire State Building</u> in <u>New York City</u>.

CAPITALS

Exercise 27.1

Underline the first letter of those words that need to be capitalized. The first one has been done for you.

1. <u>I</u> asked my uncle <u>B</u>illy, "<u>D</u>oes <u>o</u>rdinance 14 of this town set a curfew for all people under sixteen?"
2. <u>S</u>everal times this spring <u>T</u>homas and <u>J</u>ane came to <u>V</u>alley <u>F</u>orge <u>N</u>ational <u>H</u>istoric <u>P</u>ark to have a picnic with their cousins.
3. <u>W</u>ill and his sister went with their father to a candy store in <u>S</u>uburban <u>S</u>quare called <u>S</u>weet <u>P</u>leasures.
4. <u>M</u>y son <u>B</u>enjamin took <u>D</u>elta <u>A</u>ir <u>L</u>ines to <u>F</u>inland for an astronomical conference called the <u>E</u>uropean <u>W</u>eek of <u>A</u>stronomy and <u>S</u>pace <u>S</u>cience 2013.
5. <u>A</u>re you planning a trip on your wedding anniversary to the <u>L</u>ake <u>D</u>istrict in <u>E</u>ngland to see <u>D</u>ove <u>C</u>ottage, the former residence of the poet <u>W</u>illiam <u>W</u>ordsworth?

Exercise 27.2

Underline the first letter of those words that need to be capitalized.

1. <u>S</u>arah asked, "<u>I</u>s <u>O</u>xford <u>U</u>niversity or the <u>U</u>niversity of <u>P</u>aris the oldest <u>u</u>niversity in <u>E</u>urope?"
2. <u>T</u>he <u>P</u>uritan preacher <u>J</u>onathan <u>E</u>dwards went to <u>Y</u>ale when he was only fourteen years old.
3. <u>E</u>ngelbert <u>H</u>umperdinck was a <u>G</u>erman composer who studied in the <u>M</u>unich.
4. "<u>O</u>n the weekends in summer," <u>C</u>herith said, "my extended family from the <u>M</u>idwest travels to the <u>E</u>ast to visit."
5. <u>T</u>he writer <u>J</u>ohn <u>B</u>unyan was a <u>B</u>aptist lay preacher who was persecuted for preaching without a license and put in prison, where he wrote his famous allegories.

Grammar and Punctuation 28
Titles

You may remember that quotation marks are used to show the beginning and end of what someone has said. They also are used to mark titles of smaller works, such as poems, songs, articles, short stories, sermons and essays. Longer works, such as books, magazines, newspapers, journals, plays, and long poems, are underlined or written in italics. Certain special books such as the Bible and documents such as the Declaration of Independence, the Bill of Rights and the Constitution are so well known that they do not need to be marked off. They are, however, capitalized.

In addition to being highlighted by quotation marks or underlining, titles are also marked off in another way: the important words are capitalized. However, smaller words, such as *a*, *an*, *and*, *in* and *the*, are not capitalized (unless they begin the title).

Look at the following titles and notice what words are capitalized and which are not. Also notice the quotation marks, underlining and the placement of punctuation.

Example Sentences with Titles

- Last year I read William Wordsworth's "Expostulation and Reply."
- In what year was Leo Tolstoy's short story "Alyosha the Pot" written?
- I enjoyed Christopher Morley's essay "Sitting in the Barber's Chair," which appears in his book *Mince Pie*.
- The preacher Charles Haddon Spurgeon wrote "The Duty of Remembering the Poor" in order to bring to mind the Christian's duty to help those who have less. He takes his ideas from the Bible.
- <u>Charlotte's Web</u> by E. B. White is a children's book about a pig named Wilbur and his spider friend named Charlotte.

TITLES

Exercise 28.1

Put quotation marks around the titles of the smaller works and underline the larger works.

1. Written for children, Nathaniel Hawthorne's <u>Grandfather's Chair</u> contains some entertaining stories about New England history.

2. Next year my brother will be reading the <u>Odyssey</u>, which is a long epic poem about a prince trying to sail home.

3. Have you ever read John Keats' short poem "Ode to a Grecian Urn"?

4. Sarah Jewett wrote a moral tale on gossip and foolish talk titled "An Arrow in a Sunbeam."

5. One of the most popular books of all time is John Bunyan's <u>Pilgrim's Progress</u>.

6. The original title of his journal article was "Things in Space and Time."

7. I enjoyed reading the article "Saving Money on a Shoestring Budget," which I found in the new magazine <u>Household Goods</u>.

8. John Bunyan wrote other allegorical books, including "Mr. Bad Man" and "The Holy War."

9. One of the most famous sermons of American history is Jonathan Edward's "Sinners in the Hands of an Angry God."

10. One of Anthony Trollope's early novels, <u>The Warden</u>, deals with a humble and quiet minor church official who feels that he must resign his position.

Grammar and Punctuation 29
End Marks and Abbreviations

A punctuation mark helps us read and understand a sentence. Although there are many punctuation marks that can be used, the first that you must learn are the end marks, which include the period, the exclamation point and the question mark. These punctuation marks are written for you below:

- . (period)
- ! (exclamation point)
- ? (question mark)

For sentences that show strong feeling, an exclamation point is used. The exclamation point is made up of a line and a dot. Questions end in question marks, shown above. A period is used at the end of a sentence that is not a question. A period, you will notice, looks like a dot, which is placed on the line. Periods are used for other things as well. They are used for initials and abbreviations. Abbreviations are shortened ways of writing words. Many abbreviations are for titles of people and long names of organizations. Common abbreviations include those of Latin words, such as *etc.* for *et cetera* (meaning "and others").

Examples of Initials

- The American-born poet T. S. Eliot (Thomas Stearns Eliot) had worked as a banker and a school teacher.
- The first two initials of the famous essayist and author children's books E. B. White stand for Elwyn Brooks.

Examples of Abbreviations

ABBREVIATION	FULL WORD OR PHRASE
Mr.	"mister"
Mrs.	"missus"
Dr.	Doctor
Pa.	Pennsylvania
Conn.	Connecticut
Matt.	Matthew (a book in the Bible)
p.	page (*pagina*)
pp.	pages (*paginae*)
e.g.	for example (*exempli gratia*)
i.e.	that is (*id est*)
etc.	and others (*et cetera*)
cf.	compare with (*confer*)
AM	in the morning (*ante meridiem*)
PM	in the afternoon or evening (*post meridiem*)
BC	before Christ
AD	in the year of the Lord (*anno Domini*)
a.k.a.	also known as
US	United States
OED	Oxford English Dictionary

Grammar and Punctuation 30
Run-ons

When two or more sentences are combined without using correct punctuation or conjunctions, the result is a run-on sentence.

Run-on Sentence

The company was relocating to Michigan Mr. Thomas was not ready to move.

The above sentence is a run-on because there are two sentences that are joined together without using a conjunction or punctuation. The run-on may be corrected in several ways, including the following:

- Breaking up the sentence using a period
- Using a coordinating conjunction, such as *and* or *but*
- Using a subordinating conjunction, such as *while* or *because*
- Using a semicolon

A comma *cannot* correct a run-on sentence. Two sentences joined together with a commas make a special kind of run-on called a **comma splice**.

You will be learning about semicolons beginning on page 80.

Possible Corrections

The company was relocating to Michigan**.** Mr. Thomas was not ready to move. (Sentence was corrected by adding a period to divide the two sentences.)

The company was relocating to Michigan, **but** Mr. Thomas was not ready to move. (Sentence was corrected by adding the coordinating conjunction *but*.)

Although his company was relocating to Michigan, Mr. Thomas was not ready to move. (Sentence was corrected by adding the subordinating conjunction *although*.)

RUN-ONS

The company was relocating to Michigan; Mr. Thomas was not ready to move. (Sentence was corrected by adding the semicolon.)

Remember that a run-on is not just "a long sentence," but results from not using the proper conjunctions or punctuation. It is possible to write a sentence that runs the length of a 300-page book without creating a run-on!

Exercise 30.1

Correct the following run-ons by breaking up the sentence or using conjunctions.

1. Yesterday John found a collie by the curb; he didn't have a leash and he didn't know who owned him.

2. Water was scarce in that desert country, so our guide made sure that we drank a lot of water during the tour.

3. My mother bought some food items for the party since many people were coming.

4. Cherith and Sarah are not going to be there at the picnic tomorrow; they will be with their mothers at a church meeting.

5. Harry didn't want to travel alone, so they decided to take one car to the camp.

Grammar and Punctuation 31
Semicolons

You have already learned that commas are used to show a pause in speech and to avoid confusion. You also learned that periods are used to show the end of a sentence. The **semicolon** is a punctuation mark much like the comma and period. In fact, it even looks like both! It looks like a period above the line and a comma underneath (;). Semicolons join two sentences that are closely related. The semicolon almost acts as a coordinating conjunction (replacing *and* or *but*). Comma splices can often be corrected by using a semicolon.

Comma splice
George is a widely acclaimed artist, he won several awards for his oil paintings this year alone.

Corrected   George is a widely acclaimed artist; he won several awards for his oil paintings this year alone.

Semicolons also are used to make a sentence less confusing when there are a lot of commas, as in the example below:

For his hiking trip along the Sierra Nevada, Benjamin had to bring a lot of things, including a tent, which was lent to him by an astronomy professor; a lot of food, such as **dehydrated** meats and vegetables, energy bars, and tea; some clothing for the colder climate; and a small first-aid kit.

Words such as *however, on the other hand, therefore, consequently,* and *otherwise* require a semicolon before them when they are used to connect ideas in sentences. Do not use a comma before these words when they are connecting two sentences; if you do, you will create a comma splice. The words are almost always followed by a comma.

Catherine will always be my friend; however, she has moved and I doubt that our friendship will be as close as it has been.

SEMICOLONS

You may use commas with words such as *however* and *therefore* when they are not connecting sentences. Just read what comes before and after the word. If both are sentences, you need a semicolon. If they are not, you must use a comma.

Jane knew the answer; however, she did not want to speak up.

Jane, however, did not want to speak up.

Exercise 31.1

Memorize the three uses for semicolons:

- To connect sentences that are related
- To replace commas in a sentence to make it less confusing
- Before the words *however, therefore, otherwise,* etc. when they are used to connect sentences

Exercise 31.2

Correct the following sentences using semicolons.

1. John is such a hard worker on the farm; he is a responsible boy and will never leave a job undone.

2. If you see a sale on white button-down shirts, buy one; otherwise, I will make a purchase later.

3. It's important to work hard; on the other hand, it is important to know when to take a break.

4. Even though we warned her about the effects of caffeine, Maddy drank tea all day; consequently she was unable to fall asleep.

5. Many of us will go out to get some baseball practice, including Billy, the brother of my friend James; Sam, who will bring the bats; Tom and his father, who will drive us to the field; and Harry, my cousin from Iowa.

6. Tom will be going to the park tomorrow; the next day he will come to my house.

7. Sam was working; his sister was playing.

8. I wanted to help him; however, he said that he could do it himself.

9. I spent most of my budgeted money on food this month; therefore, I will not have money to buy any new clothes for the fall.

10. David is not afraid of heights; however, his sister is terrified of even climbing several rungs of a ladder.

Grammar and Punctuation 32
Comprehensive Review

Exercise 32.1

Circle the choice the correctly completes the sentence.

1. A ____ is that part of the sentence that usually follows the subject and gives information about what the subject is or does.
   a) verb
   (b) predicate
   c) modifier

2. ____ are NOT necessary in a sentence.
   a) Subjects
   b) Verbs
   (c) Modifiers

3. Verbs that add the suffix *-ed* to make the past and past participle are called ____.
   a) active verbs
   (b) regular verbs
   c) subjunctive moods

4. An incomplete sentence is called a ____.
   (a) fragment
   b) run-on
   c) predicate

5. The word *they* is an example of ____.
   (a) a subjective case personal pronoun
   b) an objective case personal pronoun
   c) an indefinite pronoun

6. A ____ names a person, place, thing or idea.
   (a) noun
   b) predicate
   c) subjective case personal pronoun

7. ____ is not a linking verb.
   a) *Were*
   b) *Is*
   (c) *In*

8. A helping verb always comes ____ a main verb.
   (a) before
   b) after

9. A verb is in the ____ voice when the subject is not doing the action of the main verb.
   a) subjective
   (b) active
   c) passive

10. The ____ is used for verbs expressing wishes and hypothetical situations.
    (a) subjunctive mood
    b) indicative mood
    c) passive voice

Exercise 32.2

Circle the choice the correctly completes the sentence.

1. The plural form of the noun *deer* is ____.
   a) *deers*
   b) *deeren*
   (c) *deer*

   There are two people on the door step.

2. The subject of the sentence above is ____.
   a) *there*
   b) *two*
   (c) *people*

COMPREHENSIVE REVIEW

3. The word *we* is ____.
   a) an indefinite pronoun
   (b) a subjective case personal pronoun
   c) an objective case personal pronoun

4. What noun follows a linking verb and renames the subject?
   a) a subject
   (b) a predicate nominative
   c) an indefinite pronoun

5. A predicate adjective describes ____.
   (a) the subject
   b) an adverb
   c) a noun which it comes before

6. What part of speech does an adjective modify?
   a) verb
   b) adverb
   (c) noun

Everyone took ____ seat by the fire.

7. What word would BEST fit the blank in the sentence above?
   (a) his
   b) their
   c) theirs

8. The word *because* is a ____.
   a) coordinating conjunction
   (b) subordinating conjunction
   c) preposition

9. The word *and* is a ____.
   (a) coordinating conjunction
   b) subordinating conjunction
   c) preposition

10. ____ often represent a pause in speech.
    a) conjunctions
    (b) commas
    c) prepositions

Exercise 32.3

Circle the correct choice.

1. An apostrophe is used for the following EXCEPT ____.
   a) to show possession
   b) for contractions
   (c) to make a word plural

   We went into the ____ stall.

2. Which of the following correctly fits the blank of the above sentence?
   a) oxens
   b) oxens'
   (c) oxen's

3. Which of the following sentences writes the title of Robert Frost's short poem correctly?
   a) We read Robert Frost's *The Road Not Taken*.
   b) We read Robert Frost's *The Road not taken*.
   (c) We read Robert Frost's "The Road Not Taken."

4. Which of the following sentences uses capitals correctly?
   a) Last Spring my teacher Mr. John Wilson went west to see his father in Columbus, Ohio and returned on Memorial day.
   b) Evi wanted to join the Havertown stamp club, but it met on Thursdays when she has her piano lesson.
   (c) The President of the United States and several diplomats traveled to France to speak to the current president about the recent trade agreement.

COMPREHENSIVE REVIEW

5. Which of the following sentences does NOT have correct punctuation?
   a) John slept; his sister Mary played.
   b) Mr. Thomas and his wife knew what was wrong with the house: it was crooked!
   (c)) Bill had a lot to read, he wished he had done some of his homework on Wednesday.

Exercise 32.4

Match the abbreviation in the right-hand column with its English meaning in the left-hand column. The first one has been done for you.

a) that is   _e_ 6. Mr.
b) in the morning   _j_ 7. etc.
c) in the evening   _d_ 8. pp.
d) pages   _b_ 9. AM
e) Mister   _c_ 10. PM
f) Pennsylvania   _i_ 11. e.g.
g) in the year of our Lord _a_ 12. i.e.
h) compare with   _f_ 13. Pa.
i) for example   _h_ 14. cf.
j) and others   _g_ 15. AD

POETRY AND POETICS

Poetry and Poetics 1
What a Poem Looks Like

You may have noticed that poems are very different from "regular" kinds of writing—chapter books, modern plays, essays, newspaper articles and stories. One difference is that regular writing, called *prose*, looks different from poetry. One kind of poem, called a shape poem, illustrates this very well. A shape poem, also called pattern poetry, is shaped into a recognizable object, such as the wings of a bird or an altar of sacrifice. The most famous shape poems in English are "Easter Wings" and "The Altar," both written by George Herbert. Shape poems, however, are rather rare in English poetry.

> These poems by George Herbert are printed on pages 94 and 95.

A more commonly noticed difference in appearance between prose and poetry is that the one is divided into paragraphs, while the other is divided up into *stanzas*. Paragraphs in prose are divided by indentations, or spaces before every first line. There is one main idea for each paragraph. When a writer begins a new idea, he must begin a new paragraph. Stanzas of poetry, however, are not divided by indentations, but are separated by spaces between them. Look at the following poem by Emily Dickinson, titled "Dawn." Can you tell how many stanzas there are in the poem?

> When night is almost done,
> And sunrise grows so near
> That we can touch the spaces,
> It's time to smooth the hair
>
> And get the dimples ready,
> And wonder we could care
> For that old faded midnight
> That frightened but an hour.

There are exactly two stanzas in "Dawn," and each of the stanzas contains four lines. You will notice that after the fourth line of the first stanza there is a space to separate it from the second. You will also notice that the lines of the poem do not extend to the very right of the page as they do in prose. Although some lines of poetry may be longer than the lines in this poem, generally they are much shorter than the width of a page. The American poet Oliver Wendell Holmes once said in so many words that the length of a line is the length of what the poet may naturally say without taking a breath. Read Dickinson's poem out loud yourself and see if you think Holmes is right.

In addition to stanzas and line length, poems are different from prose works in that they often are much shorter and sometimes contain unusual punctuation. A twentieth-century American poet named E. E. Cummings made his trademark in the placement of commas, periods and words as well as his use of lower case letters (he didn't use capitals). Some believe that these strange aspects of his poetry forced the reader to pay closer attention to what he was trying to communicate. Others believe it was a gimmick or trick that did not serve much use. Whatever the case, it certainly has made him stand out from other poets. But there are more important differences than how the poem appears on the page that we will discuss later.

One of the most famous poems written by the modern American poet William Carlos Williams is "This Is Just to Say." Although it is written as a three-stanza poem, it really reads like a hastily written note that would be taped on the door of a refrigerator. It consists of three separate sentences, in which the speaker says that he has taken some plums out of the "icebox," or refrigerator, and eaten them and then says that he is sorry with an explanation that he could not stop himself from taking them, as they were so "sweet" and "cold." If it had been written out as prose, extending to the right end of the page, "This Is Just to Say" would seem like an ordinary note. However, as it is written out in stanzas with very short lines and unusual punctuation, the reader is encouraged to think beyond the poem's obvious meaning. Do the plums represent something else? What does the speaker mean when he says the plums were "sweet" and "cold"? Is he saying stolen pleasures are sweet? Is the speaker calling the person that he is writing the note to "sweet" but "cold"?

One of the most remarkable aspects of "This Is Just to Say" is what happens when a reader reads it. Basically, three common sentences are put into stanzas with short lines and *voilà*, the work becomes a poem—and one of the most popular and talked about poems of the twentieth century! Williams' poem is a good illustration of the common understanding of poetry's power to suggest something other than what it says on the surface—to go beyond the obvious. While prose is direct and says what it means, readers expect poetry to be *suggestive*. "This Is Just to Say" may not be the most beautiful poem, but it is a clever poem. Williams was able to use the readers' expectations regarding poetic form to transform his ordinary, nothing-special-about-it refrigerator note into poetry!

Exercise 1.1

Be able to answer the following questions orally.

1. Mention specific differences between prose and poetry as it appears on the page.

2. What are some examples of prose works?

3. Who was Oliver Wendell Holmes and how did he explain the length of lines of poetry on the page?

4. What is so unusual about E. E. Cummings' poetry? Read "In Just" by E. E. Cummings and write down three examples of some of the unusual aspects discussed in this lesson.

5. What is so strange about William Carlos Williams' poem? Is it prose or poetry? Explain your opinion.

Exercise 1.2

Write out a simple note to a family member or friend and write it in stanzas, using short line and unusual punctuation. Show this simple note to someone calling it a poem, and ask what it means. Do not reveal that you have written it.

Easter Wings
By George Herbert

Lord, who createdst man in wealth and store,
Though foolishly he lost the same,
Decaying more and more,
Till he became
Most poor:
With thee
O let me rise
As larks, harmoniously,
And sing this day thy victories:
Then shall the fall further the flight in me.

My tender age in sorrow did begin:
And still with sicknesses and shame
Thou didst so punish sin,
That I became
Most thin.
With thee
Let me combine
And feel this day thy victory
For, if I imp my wing on thine,
Affliction shall advance the flight in me.

The Altar
By George Herbert

A broken A L T A R , Lord, thy servant rears,
Made of a heart, and cemented with tears:
    Whose parts are as thy hand did frame;
    No workman's tool hath touched the same.
        A H E A R T alone
        Is such a stone,
        As nothing but
        Thy pow'r doth cut.
        Wherefore each part
        Of my hard heart
        Meets in this frame,
        To praise thy name:
    That if I chance to hold my peace,
    These stones to praise thee may not cease.
O let thy blessed S A C R I F I C E be mine,
And sanctify this A L T A R to be thine.

Poetry and Poetics 2
The Language of Poetry

Another difference between prose and poetry is *language*. One easy way to illustrate that difference is by examining two accounts of an experience, one written in prose and the other written in poetry. Right below is a description of a country setting in March written by Dorothy Wordsworth. The second description is the same account, only in poetry, written by her brother William Wordsworth. As you read the two accounts, notice particularly the difference in the two writers' use of words.

Journal Entry by Dorothy Wordsworth

When I returned, I found William writing a poem descriptive of the sights and sounds we saw and heard. There was the gentle flowing of the stream, the glittering, lively lake, green fields without a living creature to be seen on them; behind us, a flat pasture with forty-two cattle feeding; to our left, the road leading to the hamlet. No smoke there, the sun shone on the bare roofs. The people were at work ploughing, harrowing, and sowing; […] a dog barking now and then, cocks crowing, birds twittering, the snow in patches at the top of the highest hills, yellow palms, purple and green twigs on the birches, ashes with their glittering stems quite bare. The hawthorn a bright green, with black stems under the oak. The moss of the oak glossy. We went on. Passed two sisters at work (they first passed us), one with two pitchforks in her hand, the other had a spade. We had come to talk with them. They laughed long after we were gone, perhaps half in wantonness, half boldness.

THE LANGUAGE OF POETRY

Lines Written in March
By William Wordsworth

The Cock is crowing,
The stream is flowing,
The small birds twitter,
The lake doth glitter,
The green field sleeps in the sun;
The oldest and youngest
Are at work with the strongest;
The cattle are grazing,
Their heads never raising;
There are forty feeding like one!

Like an army defeated
The snow hath retreated,
And now doth fare ill
On the top of the bare hill;
The Ploughboy is whooping—anon—anon:
There's joy in the mountains;
There's life in the fountains;
Small clouds are sailing,
Blue sky prevailing;
The rain is over and gone!

Poets must be more selective than prose writers in their words. Why? For many reasons. One is that a poet must say a lot more in a little space and so the language of poetry has to be more compact or condensed than that of prose. Comparing Wordsworth's description of a country scene with his sister's, you will notice that the poem (titled "Written in March") tells us only that the stream is *flowing*; it does not describe it as a *gentle stream,* as does the prose description. Wordsworth uses less description because the picture that he tried to create had to fit a much smaller "frame."

Another difference that you may have noticed is that Wordsworth's poetry uses several figures of speech, as in the statement, "The green field sleeps in the sun." When poets use figurative language, they do not mean exactly what they say. Obviously, a field cannot sleep. Perhaps what Wordsworth really means is that the expanse of green field is as still as a sleeping dog under the warm, early spring sun. (Some animals like to bask in the warm sun and will often be found sleeping in it.) Whatever the case, Wordsworth is using the word *sleep* in a figurative way. On the other hand, when Dorothy Wordsworth says in her account that there were "green fields without a living creature to be seen on them," she is being *literal*; in other words, she means exactly what she says.

Exercise 2.1

Answer the following questions in complete sentences.

1. What does the word *literal* mean?

2. What does the word *figurative* mean?

3. Find at least one figure of speech in William Wordsworth's poem (other than the use of the word *sleep*).

4. What are the two differences mentioned between the accounts of Dorothy Wordsworth and her brother?

Exercise 2.2

Write down the word in the blanks indicated by the description. The letters in the dark boxes will spell a mystery word.

1. "Easter ____" is a poem that was written by George Herbert.

2. William Carols Williams wrote a poem titled "____ Is Just to Say."

3. George Herbert's poem "The Altar" is shaped like an ____.

4. One example of prose is the modern ____.

THE LANGUAGE OF POETRY

5. ____ indicates a new paragraph in prose.

6. "Regular" writing is called ____.

7. Who said that the length of a line is the length of what the poet may naturally say without taking a breath?

8. One example of prose is the ____.

9. ____ used unusual punctuation, which some say was effective in making the reader what he was trying to say in the poem.

1. W I N G S
2. T H I S
3. A L T A R
4. P L A Y
5. I N D E N T A T I O N
6. P R O S E
7. H O L M E S
8. E S S A Y
9. C U M M I N G S

Using the letters in the dark boxes above, write down the mystery word and tell what it means.

S H A P E   P O E M

Poetry and Poetics 3
Figurative Language in Poetry

There are many kinds of figurative language. One kind is the **metaphor**, which is an indirect comparison. Suppose you heard someone say, "Don't go to that used car dealership; you can't trust the salesman. That fox sold me a real lemon." The customer would be making a comparison between a salesman and a fox, meaning that just as a fox slyly steals eggs or chickens from the henhouse, the salesman is dishonest in the way he does business. Like metaphors, similes compare two things, only the comparison made is made more direct by using the words *like* or *as*. In the statement *Like a fox, the salesman made a shady deal*, the salesman is compared to a fox in a simile because the sentence uses the word *like*.

Another figure of speech is **metonymy**, which is a word used in place of another that is closely related to it. In the sentence *The White House said that it was unwilling to compromise*, *White House* is used to refer to the President, as the President of the United States lives in the White House. Another example would be to use the word *crown* to mean "king," and *bottle* to mean "wine."

When a writer or speaker uses part of something to mean its whole, or vice versa—when he uses the whole to represent the part—he is using **synecdoche**. Saying to someone who has bought a new car, "That's a nice set of wheels!" would be using synecdoche, because part of the car (its wheels) are being used for the whole (the car). An example in which the whole represents the part is when newspaper reports say that the town came out to see the show. The reporter does not mean every person in the town without exception.

Another figure of speech is **personification**. When a writer or speaker gives human characteristic to something not human, he is using personification. You will recall that in Wordsworth's poem "Written in March," the green fields were said to be sleeping in the sun. Green fields do not sleep as people (or animals) do. You may have been able to identify some of the other figures of speech in the poem, some of which are personification. The statement that the "snow hath retreated" is an example of personification. An army retreats, but snow melts.

A figure of speech closely related to personification is the **pathetic fallacy**. When poets or writers talk about nature, such as a flower, tree, snow, or bird, as having having human feeling, they are using this figure of speech. In Wordsworth's poem, the mountains are said to be full of joy. We like to transfer our feelings to the things we see around us. When we are happy, the birds seem happy with us and their songs seem songs of joy. It is the poet, then, in "Written in March" who is joyous about the coming of spring, not the mountain.

Exercise 3.1

Be able to answer the following questions orally.

1. What is a metaphor? Give an example of a metaphor.

2. What figure of speech uses a part to represent the whole or the whole to represent a part?

3. What figure of speech is a word used in place of another that is closely related to it?

4. What figure of speech is like a metaphor but uses *like* or *as*?

Exercise 3.2

Write down the word (or part of a word) in the blanks indicated by the description. The letters in the dark boxes will spell a mystery word.

1. A simile uses the word ____ or *as* in making a comparison.

2. William Wordsworth wrote "____ in March" in response to an experience he had in the country.

3. A figure of speech in which nonhumans are given human qualities is called person____.

4. A figure of speech in which a part represents the whole or the whole represents a part.

POETRY & POETICS 3

5. The sister of William Wordsworth was named ____.

6. The figure of speech in which a part of nature, such as a tree, stream or rock, is described as having emotions such as happiness or anger is called the ____ fallacy.

7. William Carlos ____ wrote poem that reads a lot like prose, titled "This Is Just to Say."

1. L I K E
2. W R I T T E N
3. I F I C A T I O N
4. S Y N E C D O C H E
5. D O R O T H Y
6. P A T H E T I C
7. W I L L I A M S

Using the letters in the dark boxes above, write down the mystery word and tell what it means.

L I T E R A L

Poetry and Poetics 4
Irony and Oxymoron

There are several kinds of irony. Two if them—dramatic irony and situational irony—are discussed in the section "Lyman Dean's Testimonials." Another kind is verbal irony., which can rightly be called a figure of speech, as when a a poem uses verbal irony what is said is not what is meant. Suppose, for example, that there is a student who likes to boast how many books he reads. His friend, however, knows his habits, and responds, "Yes, you are a real bookworm." The friend is using verbal irony. A bookworm is someone who reads a lot, a word that does not describe the friend at all; just the opposite, he reads very little. Verbal irony, then, is a figure of speech in which a person means something opposite to what he says. When used in speech, verbal irony is called *sarcasm*.

Verbal irony is used in Robert Frost's "The Road Not Taken." Unfortunately, many readers miss the verbal irony in the last stanza and so misunderstand the meaning of the poem. In the poem, the speaker tells an experience he had in the woods. He was walking along a road, which split up into two paths, which are really basically the same. Which should he take? The speaker spends a long time deciding which, but eventually he must make up his mind, and chooses one. The other road allures him, but knows that it is unlikely that he will ever know what it was like. The poem ends this way:

> I shall be telling this with a sigh
> Somewhere ages and ages hence:
> Two roads diverged in a wood, and I—
> I took the one less traveled by,
> And that has made all the difference.

The last line is "That has made all the difference." *What* has made all the difference? The road that the speaker has taken was no different from the other. But why does he *say* it has made all the difference when it hasn't. The poet is using verbal irony to draw the reader's attention to a person's desire to rationalize. In other words, the speaker wants to believe that his decision was the better one.

See page 189 in the study guide for a discussion on rationalization.

An **oxymoron** is a figure of speech that involves clashing words—words that do not go together. Here are some examples: *little giant, civilized savage, gentle lion, good witch, foolish sage, idiot savant* (a *savant* is a very intelligent person). Using oxymorons can be quite effective in making a point by drawing the reader's attention to an apparent contradiction, or something that appears to be impossible. For example, if a poet wanted to criticize a war that he thought was senseless, he might call the nations involved in it *civilized savages*. The poet would be making a point that although the nations involved in the war are advanced in their culture and technology is civilized, they are really barbarous in taking part in a cruel and senseless war.

Exercise 4.1

Be able to answer the following questions orally.

1. What is verbal irony and how is it a figure of speech?

2. When verbal irony is used in speech, what is it called?

3. How would you use verbal irony to draw attention to the fact that you have taken a whole hour to solve a puzzle that you boasted that you could complete in one minute?

4. Think of a situation in which you could use the oxymoron *little giant* appropriately.

IRONY AND OXYMORON

Exercise 4.2

Write down the word in the blanks indicated by the description. The letters in the dark boxes will spell a mystery word.

1. It is the opposite of *literal*.
2. A brother and sister with this last name wrote an account of an experience out in the country on an early spring day.
3. A clashing combination of words is called an ____.
4. A figure of speech in which a part represents a whole or the whole represents a part.
5. A figure of speech in which a person or thing is represented by something closely related to it.

1. F **I** G U R A T I V E
2. W O **R** D S W O R T H
3. **O** X Y M O R O N
4. S Y **N** E C D O C H E
5. M E T O N **Y** M Y

Using the letters in the dark boxes above, write down the mystery word and tell what it means.

Poetry and Poetics 5
Music in Poetry

In the ancient days when poetry was sung, the music of a poem was easier to hear. Older works such as the Old English poem *Beowulf* and Homer's *Odyssey* and *Iliad* were all composed to be sung to the accompaniment of the harp, lute, or lyre. Wouldn't it be exciting to travel back in time to hear an Old English poet, called a **scop** (pronounced *shope*), singing with his early medieval harp? You would hear exciting stories about monsters, heroes and the battles that the heroes fought. You would quite likely be in the audience with the kingdom's noblemen, as the performance of the scop's poetry was high entertainment and fit for a king!

A scop was not only a singer but also a poet. He had to create, then perform. Interestingly enough, the word *scop* is related to the Old English word *scapen*, which means "to create," just as the word *poetry* comes from the Greek word *poiein*, which also means "to create." A poet, like all artists, creates things seemingly out of thin air!

We don't need, however, to go back in time to enjoy poetry. Students just need to look beyond the printed poem to the *music* and see its beauty. Singing the poems might help. Many modern poems, not originally meant to be sung, have been put to music, such as Robert Frost's "The Road Not Taken." Robert Frost (1874–1963) did not write music for his poem, though later composers have put his poetry to music. But there was already music "under the hood"—music provided by the poet which the composer drew from.

MUSIC IN POETRY

Exercise 5.1

Be able to answer the following questions orally.

1. Explain how poetry and music are "cousins."
2. What is an Old English minstrel called?
3. What does the word *poetry* literally mean in Greek?
4. In what way are the *Odyssey*, the *Iliad* and *Beowulf* alike?

Exercise 5.2

Write down the word in the blanks indicated by the description. The letters in the dark boxes will spell a mystery word.

1. Homer composed the Iliad and the ____.
2. When something is not meant literally, it is a figure of ____.
3. Oliver Wendell ____ was an American poet.
4. "Easter Wings" and "The Altar" are examples of ____.

1. O D Y S S E Y
2. S P E E C H
3. H O L M E S
4. S H A P E   P O E M S

Using the letters in the dark boxes above, write down the mystery word and tell what it means.

S C O P

107

Poetry and Poetics 6
Syllables

Another important difference between poetry and prose is not what we *see*—stanzas, length of lines, and punctuation, but what we *hear*, such as rhythm. The words that a poet uses are partly chosen for their sound and cadence, as the poet must arrange the words in patterns to create a certain kind of "music."

When studying poetry, you will need to know many words. These words may sound hard, but once you learn what they mean, they will seem not so difficult. The first "hard" word that you will be learning is the word **poetics** (*po-et-ics*). Poetics is the study of how poetry "works." In the same way that a student car mechanic looks under the hood of a car to learn how it works, a student of poetry must "look under the hood" of a poem. And just as there is a lot of interesting machinery under the hood of a car, you will be surprised to find all the interesting things found under the hood of a poem.

One word that is very important to know when studying poetry is **syllable**. We really cannot continue unless you know this word. A *syllable* is the "beat" of a word. It is made up of a vowel sound and any consonants attached to that vowel. Every syllable must have a vowel sound, but does not need a consonant sound. The word *look* has one vowel sound and one syllable. The whole word makes up the syllable. The word *belong* has two vowel sounds and two syllables. The first syllable is *be* and the second is *long*. It may be broken up this way: *be-long*. The word *historical* has four vowel sounds and four syllables: *his-tor-i-cal*. (Notice that the third syllable of this word has a vowel but no consonant.) The word with the most syllables included in *Webster's Third New International Dictionary* is:

pneumonoultramicroscopicsilicovolcanoconiosis

Can you tell how many syllables it has?

SYLLABLES

Exercise 6.1

Read the following words aloud and tell the number of syllables.

Example: good-bye
two syllables

1. forest   2
2. run   1
3. dramatically   4
4. yesterday   3
5. loose   1
6. second   2
7. hill   1
8. United States of America   9
9. mask   1
10. kitchen   2
11. Cherokee   3
12. list   1
13. listen   2
14. fascination   4
15. eventual   4

Exercise 6.2

Write down the name of a fruit that has one syllable, one that has two syllables, one that has three syllables, and one that has four syllables.

Example: three syllables
tangerine

Poetry and Poetics 7
Stress

You will notice that words themselves have a sort of music to them. The rhythm of English words is found in the syllables. Some syllables receive more **stress** than others. When words are put together, the syllables form what is called a stress pattern. If there is stress on a syllable, that means that it is said more loudly than the others.

Let's look at the word *appear* as an example. You will notice that it has two syllables: *ap-* and *-pear*. Can you tell which syllable is "louder"? It is louder on the second syllable (*-pear*) than on the first (*ap-*). We say, then, that the stress is on the second syllable of the word. If you pronounce the word with the stress on the first syllable, and the word will not sound right. The stress pattern of the word is weak–STRONG.

We often mark a stressed or strong syllable by a slash mark (/) above the syllable, and an unstressed or weak syllable by another mark (⌣). Below are some more examples of words and their stress patterns:

/ ⌣
cover

⌣ /
aside

/ ⌣ ⌣
estimate

⌣ / ⌣
encourage

⌣ ⌣ / ⌣
information

⌣ ⌣ / ⌣ ⌣
university

STRESS

Exercise 7.1

Write down the stress pattern of the following words.

Example 1: delight
⌣ /

Example 2: daring
/ ⌣

1. frosty   / ⌣
2. allow   ⌣ /
3. hunter   / ⌣
4. forest   / ⌣
5. apart   ⌣ /
6. aware   ⌣ /
7. igloo   / ⌣
8. event   ⌣ /
9. garage   ⌣ /
10. dotted / ⌣

POETRY & POETICS 7

Exercise 7.2

Write down the word in the blanks indicated by the description. The letters in the dark boxes will spell a mystery word.

1. "The ____" was written by the poet George Herbert.
2. "Easter Wings" is an example of a ____.
3. A chapter ____ is an example of prose.
4. The word *trouble* has two ____.
5. A ____ of speech is language that does not mean exactly what it says.
6. ____ is the study of how poetry works.
7. ____ is an Old English poem.
8. ____ composed an epic poem called the *Iliad*.
9. One of Homer's poems is titled the ____.
10. An Old English poet and singer was called a ____.
11. The mark / indicates that a syllable is strong or ____.

STRESS

1. A L T A R
2. S H A P E   P O E M
3. B O O K
4. S Y L L A B L E S
5. F I G U R E
6. P O E T I C S
7. B E O W U L F
8. H O M E R
9. O D Y S S E Y
10. S C O P
11. S T R E S S E D

Using the letters in the dark boxes above, write down the mystery word and tell what it means.

R O B E R T   F R O S T

Poetry and Poetics 8
Examples of Music in Poetry

In the previous lessons you learned about the rhythm in poems, which makes them very suitable for singing. Robert Frost's "The Road Not Taken" is just one example of the many, many poems that were later put into music. The composer Randall Thompson (1899–1984) included "The Road Not Taken" as just one of the several poems by Frost in a choral work titled *Frostiana*.

It would be very difficult in a short space to mention the names of the English and American poems put to music. As was stated in the previous lesson, many years ago poems were originally written primarily to be sung, such as the Medieval work, *Beowulf*. Other poems, such as the English ballads, were also originally songs. You will be learning more about ballads in a later section.

Many Christian poems were originally written to be sung as hymns or carols, such as those by Isaac Watts (1674–1748), Charles Wesley (1703–1791), and William Cowper (1731–1800). Watts, Wesley, and Cowper were poets in their own right, yet their works are mostly known through singing. The carols "Joy to the World" by Isaac Watts and "Hark! the Herald Angels Sing" are sung world wide, and William Cowper's "There is a Fountain" and "God Moves in a Mysterious Way" still enjoy wide popularity in Christian congregations.

Many popular singers and folk artists not in the classical tradition have made noble efforts to breathe new life into traditional ballads and classical poetry. Very old songs such as the "The Three Ravens," a gloomy traditional ballad about three birds of prey watching a knight die, and "Barbara Allen," a sad English ballad about a man who dies of love, are still sung by popular music artists. Not just ballads, but also many other poems never sung before have come to life through the work of popular singers, including works by poets Ogden Nash, Gerard Manley Hopkins, Christina Rossetti, E. E. Cummings and others.

EXAMPLES OF MUSIC IN POETRY

Exercise 8.1

Write down the stress pattern of the following words. Some of the words have more than two syllables, and at least one of the words has more than one stressed syllable.

Example 1: spaghetti
˘ / ˘

Example 2: carpool
/ /

1. forget ˘ /
2. pebble / ˘
3. savior / ˘
4. across ˘ /
5. escaping ˘ / ˘
6. minister / ˘ ˘
7. irritate / ˘ ˘
8. sailboat / /
9. review ˘ /
10. armchair / /

Exercise 8.2

Write down the word in the blanks indicated by the description. The letters in the dark boxes will spell a mystery word.

1. The poetry of ____ continues to be sung in Christian churches today.
2. One of Charles Wesley's most famous poems is "____! the Herald Angels Sing."
3. ____ wrote a choral work that celebrates Robert Frost's poetry.
4. "The ____ Ravens" is a traditional ballad about the death of a knight.
5. The syllables of words form a ____ pattern.

1. | C | O | W | P | E | R |
2. | H | A | R | K |
3. | T | H | O | M | P | S | O | N |
4. | T | H | R | E | E |
5. | S | T | R | E | S | S |

Using the letters in the dark boxes above, write down the mystery word and explain its significance to music and poetry.

| W | A | T | T | S |

Poetry and Poetics 9
Scansion

Although most poems aren't sung today, to enjoy a poem fully, the reader should at least read it out loud. Let us listen to the "music" of the poetry of William Wordsworth, and then look underneath its "hood." Read the poem aloud several times before you read on.

> In clouds above, the lark is heard,
> He sings his blithest and his best;
> But in this lonesome nook the bird
> Did never build his nest.

Did you notice the "rhythm" of this poem? The rhythm is called its **meter**. Simply put, the meter of a poem is its stress pattern. Finding the meter of a poem can be hard at first, but in order to appreciate a poem more fully, a reader should **scan** the poem for its meter. Scanning a poem involves finding out what syllables are stressed and what syllables are not and seeing a pattern. Finding the meter of a particular poem is called **scansion**. To scan the above lines by Wordsworth, we need to do the following:

1. Look for words that have more than one syllable.

2. Find the stressed and unstressed syllables of those words.

3. By sounding out the lines, figure out the stress pattern of the remaining words.

Let's apply these steps to the stanza above to scan it.

1. We see that the only words that have more than one syllable in the first two lines of Wordsworth's poem are *above* and *blithest*. (*Blithest* means "happiest.")

2. When we say the words, we see that the accent is on the second syllable of *above* and the first syllable of *blithest*. Thus, we pronounce the words this way: a-*bove* and *blith*-est. As you already learned, we often represent the stressed syllable with / and the unstressed or weak syllable with ⌣.

3. Now that we know the stress pattern of *above* and *blithest*, the other words may be more easily scanned. When the first line is read, what single-syllable words are stressed? This might be hard for some readers to hear. It might help, then, to remember that often a stress mark will not come right after another stress mark. You might also need to pronounce the line aloud several times in order for you to see the stress pattern. When you do, it becomes clear that there is no accent on the word *in*, but there is one on the word *clouds*. We then begin to see the pattern:

⏑ / ⏑ /
In clouds above

You see, then, that there is a pattern of syllables. Do you see that this pattern (⏑ /) is repeated two times above? The pattern involves one stress and one unstressed syllable. One set of these patterns is called a **foot**. A *foot* is one set of any kind of stress pattern. In lines of two-syllable patterns, there will be two times as many syllables as there are feet. If there are two syllables, there will be one foot. If there are four syllables, there will be two feet. The first two lines are scanned below:

⏑ / ⏑ / ⏑ / ⏑ /
In clouds above, the lark is heard,
⏑ / ⏑ / ⏑ / ⏑ /
He sings his blithest and his best…

SCANSION

Exercise 9.1

Write down the word in the blanks indicated by the description. The letters in the dark boxes will spell a mystery word.

1. An indirect comparison, as in the sentence *That problem was a piece of cake*, is called a ____.
2. The rhythm of poetry is called its ____.
3. One of Homer's poems is titled ____.
4. To ____ a poem means to find its stress pattern.
5. The most famous Old English poem is titled ____.

1. M E T A **P** H O R
2. M E T **E** R
3. **O** D Y S S E Y
4. **S** C A N
5. B **E** O W U L F

Using the letters in the dark boxes above, write down the mystery word and tell what it means.

P R O S E

Exercise 9.2

Scan the following lines of poetry and divide the lines into feet. Write down the foot, or stress pattern, that is repeated in the lines.

Example: My heart ˘/ is like ˘/ a sing ˘/ ing bird /

Whose nest ˘/ is in ˘/ a wa ˘/ tered shoot. /   ˘/

1. Forgive ˘/ the song ˘/ that falls ˘/ so low /
   Beneath ˘/ the grat ˘/ itude ˘/ I owe. /   ˘/

2. The hope ˘/ I dreamed ˘/ of was ˘/ a dream, /
   Was but ˘/ a dream; ˘/ and now ˘/ I wake. /   ˘/

3. Piping /˘ down the /˘ valleys /˘ wild, /
   Piping /˘ songs of /˘ pleasant /˘ glee. /   /˘

4. Curious, /˘˘ beautiful /˘˘ little /˘ one, /
   Mother is /˘˘ gathering /˘˘ one by /˘ one /
   Little /˘˘ magnolias /˘˘ just for /˘ you. /   /˘

Poetry and Poetics 10
Iamb

There are a variety of stress patterns that may appear in a line of poetry. One of the most common is the pattern ⌣ /. It is called an **iamb**. One pair of these syllables is called an **iambic foot**. Read aloud the four lines below taken from Christina Rossetti's poem "May" and take notice of the stressed and unstressed syllables.

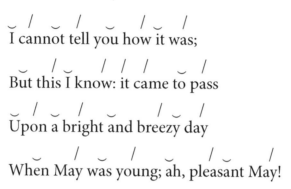

Although only four lines have been printed, this weak–STRONG pattern continues throughout the whole poem. Poems that contain this pattern are called **iambic poems**. Iambic poems are the most common poems written in English meter.

Exercise 10.1

Scan the following words and write down whether they are iambic or not iambic.

1. create   iambic
2. hungry   not
3. yellow   not
4. decide   iambic
5. water   not

6. nutty   not
7. puppy   not
8. appear   iambic
9. hiccup   not
10. aside   iambic

Exercise 10.2

Scan the following excerpt of a poem and answer the questions that come after it.

⏑ / ⏑ / ⏑ / ⏑ /
We passed the school where children played,

⏑ / ⏑ / ⏑ /
Their lessons scarcely done;

⏑ / ⏑ / ⏑ / ⏑ /
We passed the fields of gazing grain,

⏑ / / ⏑ /
We passed the setting sun.

1. How many syllables are there in the first line?
    a) two
    b) four
    c) six
    (d) eight
    e) ten

2. What is the stress pattern of the word "children" in line 1?
    a) iambic
    (b) not iambic

3. How many feet are there in the first line?
    a) two
    b) three
    (c) four
    d) five
    e) six

IAMB

4. What is the stress pattern of the word "setting" in line 4?
    a) iambic
    ⓑ) not iambic

5. What is the stress pattern of the last line?
    a) ⌣⌣/⌣⌣/
    b) /⌣/⌣/⌣
    ⓒ) ⌣/⌣/⌣/
    d) /⌣⌣/⌣⌣
    e) /⌣⌣⌣/⌣

Poetry and Poetics 11
Greek Words in Poetry

A line of poetry may have more than one foot or stress pattern, such as the iamb (⌣ /). A line can have two, three, four, five—up to eight or nine feet. To name these lines of different length, we use Greek words, as early English scholars looked to the ancient Greek writers who had written poetry many years before English was even spoken. The Greek words may at first sound difficult, but they really just refer to numbers of feet. Before we go over the names of these lines, it might be good to go over the Greek root words to aid the learning and memory of the words.

In English we have some common words that use the Greek root *mono-*. *Monk* is such a word. It names a person who lives *alone*. *Monotonous* is another word with this root. It describes anything that does not vary from *one* tone, such as in the phrase "reading in a monotonous voice." *Mono-*, therefore, means "one."

The Greek root *di-* means "two." Unfortunately, we do not have many common words using this root, as most English words containing a root for "two" come from the Latin root, *bi-*, such as *bicycle* and *binoculars*. The roots are similar enough, though, that it may help you to learn the word *dimeter*.

A *triangle*, you may know already, is a figure made up of three sides; the root *tri-* means "three." The other roots are *tetra-* ("four"), *penta-* ("five"), *hexa-* ("six"), *hepta-* ("seven"), and *octo-* ("eight").

Now that you have learned these roots, it will be easier to learn and memorize the Greek names given to lines of poetry. The roots indicating the number are all followed by the word *meter*, which literally means "measure."

Name of meter	Number of feet
monometer	one foot
dimeter	two feet
trimeter	three feet

GREEK WORDS IN POETRY

tetrameter	four feet
pentameter	five feet
hexameter	six feet
heptameter	seven feet
octameter	eight feet

Exercise 11.1

Tell whether the following words are iambic or not.

6. singer   not
7. kerchief   not
8. bassoon   iambic
9. tickle   not
10. water   not
11. rely   iambic
12. ketchup   not
13. before   iambic
14. baboon   iambic
15. reason   not

Exercise 11.2

Write down the Greek roots used in the following words and their meaning. Then, look up the words in a dictionary and write down the meanings of the words themselves.

Example: Pentagon
penta- (five)   The Pentagon is a building used for military purposes in Washington, DC. It has five sides.

1. octopus   oct- (eight)
2. dilemma   di- (two)
3. triangle   tri- (three)
4. tetrahedron   tetra- (four)
5. octogenarian   octo- (eight)
6. tripod   tri- (three)
7. hexagon   hexa- (six)
8. monarch   mono- (one)
9. monogram   mono- (one)
10. trivet   tri- (three)

Poetry and Poetics 12
Meter

When identifying the meter of a line of poetry, usually two pieces of information are given: the stress pattern and line length. The only stress pattern that you have learned so far is the iambic stress pattern (⌣ /). You have learned eight terms that identify the length of a line of poetry: *monometer, dimeter,* etc. A line of poetry that has only *one* iambic foot, then, is called *iambic monometer*. A line of two iambic feet is called *iambic dimeter*. A line of three iambic feet is called *iambic trimeter*— and so on.

There is a special name given to an unrhymed poem written completely in iambic pentameter, or a line of five iambic feet. It is called **blank verse**. Shakespeare wrote his plays in blank verse. The line below is from a funeral speech given by Mark Antony in Shakespeare's tragedy *Julius Caesar*. In the beginning of his speech, Antony grabs the attention of his audience by saying:

Friends, Romans, countrymen, lend me your ears.

If you count the number of syllables of the above line, or most lines in *Julius Caesar,* you will notice that there are ten. Iambic pentameter poems typically have lines of five feet and ten syllables.

In strict iambic meters, the lines will have twice as many syllables as feet. This makes sense because an iambic foot is made up of two syllables, the first unstressed, the second stressed. If there are two iambic feet, there are four syllables. If there are three iambic feet, there are six syllables.

Let us now look at some iambic lines that show the different meters. Below is a chart of lines of varying length, beginning with monometer. Read the lines and observe the stressed syllables (marked with an acute accent, /) and unstressed syllables (marked with a breve symbol, ⌣). Count the number of syllables and notice that the there are twice as many syllables as there are feet. Each foot is separated by a perpendicular line (|).

METER

Lines Illustrating the Different Meters

monometer (one foot)

My hĕart!

dimeter (two feet)

Thĕ babe | lŏoked up.

trimeter (three feet)

Hĕ went | tŏ see | thĕ wind.

tetrameter (four feet)

Whŏ knows | thĕ trou|blĕ of | hĕr heart?

pentameter (five feet)

Hĕr sing|ĭng made | thĕ birds | tŏ stop | ănd hear.

hexameter (six feet)

Ănd she | wăs sick | wĭth fe|vĕr, cry|ĭng for | hĕr boy.

heptameter (seven feet)

Ĭt's true: | thĕ one | whŏ knows | thĕ an|swĕr of|tĕn will | nŏt speak.

octameter (eight feet)

Ăt e|vĕntide | shĕ went | tŏ watch | thĕ ship | cŏme in, | ănd then | ĭt came.

POETRY & POETICS 12

Exercise 12.1

In this exercise you will be looking at stanzas of poems and scanning each of the lines. Do the following:

- Scan the lines by writing the symbols that mark the stressed and unstressed syllables.

- Write down the number of feet and syllables of each line

- Write down the name of the meter of the poem.

Example:

⏑ / ⏑ / ⏑ / ⏑ /
The sun descending in the west,   8 syllables, 4 feet
⏑ / ⏑ / ⏑ /
The evening star does shine;   6 syllables, 3 feet
⏑ / ⏑ / ⏑ / ⏑ /
The birds are silent in their nest,   8 syllables, 4 feet
⏑ / ⏑ / ⏑ /
And I must seek for mine.   6 syllables, 3 feet

(iambic tetrameter)

1. ⏑ / ⏑ /
   And am not I   4 syllables, 2 feet
   ⏑ / ⏑ /
   A fly like thee?   4 syllables, 2 feet
   ⏑ / ⏑ /
   Or art not thou   4 syllables, 2 feet
   ⏑ / ⏑ /
   A man like me?   4 syllables, 2 feet

   (iambic dimeter)

2. ⏑ / ⏑ / ⏑ / ⏑ /
   I dreamt a dream! What can it mean?   4 syllables, 2 feet
   ⏑ / ⏑ / ⏑ / ⏑ /
   And that I was a maiden Queen.   4 syllables, 2 feet

   (iambic tetrameter)

METER

3. The mŏdést Rose pŭts fórth ă thórn,   8 syllables, 4 feet
   Thĕ húmblĕ shéep ă thréat'nĭng hórn.   8 syllables, 4 feet

   (iambic tetrameter)

4. Swĕet dréams ŏf pléasănt stréams   6 syllables, 3 feet
   Bў háppy̆, sílĕnt, móonў béams!   8 syllables, 4 feet

   (iambic trimeter and tetrameter)

5. Ŏur tóngues wĕre máde tŏ bléss thĕ Lórd,   8 syllables, 4 feet
   Ănd nót spĕak íll ŏf mén: 6 syllables, 3 feet
   Whĕn óthĕrs gíve ă ráilĭng wórd,   8 syllables, 4 feet
   Wĕ múst nŏt ráil ăgáin.   6 syllables, 3 feet

   (iambic tetrameter and trimeter)

Exercise 12.2

Write down the word from the word bank that fits the description given. The first one has been done for you.

Word Bank: trimeter, ~~poetics~~, iamb, octometer, prose, tetrameter, foot, blank verse, scansion, pentameter

1. The study of poetry   poetics
2. "Regular" writing, such as a newspaper article or an essay
3. An unrhymed iambic pentameter poem   blank verse
4. Reading a poem for its stress and rhythm   scansion
5. A foot that contains the stress pattern ⌣ /   iamb
6. Describing a poem or a line of poetry that has four feet   tetrameter
7. A division of a line of poetry that contains a pattern of stressed and unstressed syllables   foot

8. Describing a poem or a line of poetry that has five feet   pentameter

9. Describing a poem or a line of poetry that has three feet   trimeter

10. Describing a poem or a line of poetry that has eight feet   octameter

Poetry and Poetics 13
Trochee

You have already learned about iambic meter, which has the pattern ⌣ / . There is another stress pattern that you have already seen—for example, in the exercise on page 121—but just haven't learned the name of. It is called the **trochaic foot**. The trochaic foot has a stress pattern that is opposite to that of the iambic. That means that the first syllable is stressed and the second is unstressed: STRONG–weak (/ ⌣). A trochaic foot is called a **trochee**. Words such as *happy, parent, larger* and *fancy* are all trochees. Even though the most common stress pattern in poetry is iambic, most two-syllable words in the English language are trochaic.

Exercise 13.1

Indicate whether the following words are iambic or trochaic.

1. pillow   trochaic
2. drastic   trochaic
3. caress   iambic
4. funny   trochaic
5. today   iambic
6. arrange   iambic
7. under   trochaic
8. above   iambic
9. choosy   trochaic
10. swindle   trochaic

Exercise 13.2

Indicate whether the following lines are iambic or trochaic.

1. Even Tommy knew the answer.   trochaic
2. Do not forget to take the trash outside.   iambic
3. Although my mother said he wasn't coming, David came.   iambic
4. Just in case she sees you, hide behind this pillar.   trochaic

Poetry and Poetics 14
Spondee

Another stress pattern is the **spondaic foot** (called a **spondee**) involving two stressed beats (/ /). Words such as *toothpaste, airplane, hairpin,* and *flashlight* have this stress pattern. Spondees are sparingly used. There are very few long lines in poetry that are purely spondaic. Below is a summary of all the stress patterns we have gone over so far.

Name of meter	Stress pattern
iamb (iambic meter)	⌣ /
trochee (trochaic meter)	/ ⌣
spondee (spondaic meter)	/ /

Exercise 14.1

Scan the following words and tell whether they are iambic or trochaic.

1. looking   trochaic
2. apple   trochaic
3. beside   iambic
4. alive   iambic
5. atop   iambic
6. triple   trochaic
7. awake   iambic
8. virtue   trochaic
9. between   iambic
10. manly   trochaic

Exercise 14.2

Scan the following words and tell whether they are iambic, trochaic or spondaic.

1. friendship   trochaic
2. serene   iambic
3. cheesecake   spondaic
4. nature   trochaic
5. mature   iambic
6. pickle   trochaic
7. stroller   trochaic
8. trailer   trochaic
9. amazed   iambic
10. windshield   spondaic

Poetry and Poetics 15
Catalectic and Acatalectic

> Oh for boyhood's time of June,
> Crowding years in one brief moon,
> When all things I heard or saw,
> Me, their master, waited for.

The above four lines are from John Greenleaf Whittier's poem "The Barefoot Boy." To scan the poem, remember we first look at the words with more than one syllable: *boyhood, crowding, master,* and *waited*. If we say the words aloud, we can recognize that all of them are trochaic. The first syllable of each of these words is stressed, while the second is unstressed.

/ ˘
boy-hood's

/ ˘
crowd-ing

/ ˘
mas-ter

/ ˘
wait-ed

We can see that the trochaic pattern continues with the words after *boyhood's*. We would never say "time OF June" with the stress on *of*. In fact, prepositions of one syllable, such as *of, on, in, for,* and *to* are rarely stressed. The two syllables before *boyhood's* also fit the pattern, and so the entire line follows the trochaic (/ ˘) pattern:

/ ˘ / ˘ / ˘ /
Oh for boyhood's time of June,

Did you notice that we have an extra stressed syllable at the end of the line above? We don't have four full trochaic feet—we have three and a half. This happens often in trochaic meter. It's natural to want to end a line on a stressed syllable.

We have a special name for a line in poetry that has an incomplete or imperfect foot at the end: **catalectic**. A trochaic line that is catalectic will always end with a stressed syllable. A trochaic line without that extra beat is called **acatalectic**. An acatalectic line in trochaic meter always ends with an unstressed syllable. Acatalectic lines in trochaic meter are less usual, as, again, it seems more natural to end a line with a stressed syllable.

catalectic   having an incomplete last foot in a line of poetry

acatalectic   having a complete last foot in a line of poetry

Iambic lines may also be catalectic, or have an imperfect foot at the end. Let us look at two lines from a poem by Emily Dickinson:

> If I can stop one heart from breaking,
> I shall not live in vain.

The above two lines are iambic. The first would be scanned this way:

$$\smile / \smile / \smile / \smile / \smile$$
If I can stop one heart from breaking,

You will notice that the line has four iambic feet with an extra unstressed syllable. Because the last foot is missing an accented beat, we call it an incomplete or imperfect foot. The first line of the poem, then, is a catalectic iambic line. Let us, however, examine the next line of the poem:

$$\smile / \smile / \smile /$$
I shall not live in vain.

This line is acatalectic because there is not an imperfect or incomplete foot at the end of the line. The whole poem appears below. The catalectic lines are indicated by an asterisk (*), while the acatalectic lines are indicated by a dagger (†). All the lines are iambic.

> * If I can stop one heart from breaking,
> † I shall not live in vain.
> * If I can ease one life the aching,
> † Or cool one pain,
> * Or help one fainting robin
> † Unto his nest again,
> † I shall not live in vain.

CATALECTIC AND ACATALECTIC

Exercise 15.1

Write down the word in the blanks indicated by the description. The letters in the dark boxes will spell a mystery word.

1. A poetic foot with the pattern / ⌣ is called a ____ foot.
2. A line of poetry with five feet is called a ____.
3. It is the "measure" of poetry.
4. A word that forms a spondee has two stressed ____.
5. A line of poetry with two feet is called a ____.
6. A line of iambs that ends with an stressed syllable is ____.

1. T R O C H A **I** C
2. P E N T **A** M E T E R
3. **M** E T E R
4. S Y L L A **B** L E S
5. C **O** U P L E T
6. A **C** A T A L E C T I C

Using the letters in the dark boxes above, write down the mystery word and tell what it means.

I A M B I C

Exercise 15.2

Match the word or root in the left-hand column with its definition or description in the right-hand column. The first one has been done for you.

a) prose

b) dimeter

c) tri-

d) Iliad

e) scan

f) octo-

g) blank verse

h) Beowulf

i) scop

j) catalectic

_f_ 1. a Greek root word that means "eight"

_h_ 2. an Old English poem

_d_ 3. a poem by Homer

_a_ 4. A newspaper article is an example of ____.

_i_ 5. an Old English poet

_e_ 6. to read for a poem's meter

_j_ 7. a trochaic line with a stress at the end

_g_ 8. an unrhymed poem in iambic pentameter

_b_ 9. a line two feet long

_c_ 10. a Greek root that means "three"

Poetry and Poetics 16
Anapestic

In your anthology (page 386) there is a poem by George Gordon Byron titled "The Destruction of Sennacherib." It has a more unusual stress pattern, called **anapestic**. The poem is probably the most famous example of this type of meter. The first four lines are written below.

> The Assyrian came down like the wolf on the fold,
> And his cohorts were gleaming in purple and gold;
> And the sheen of his spears was like stars on the sea
> When the blue wave rolls nightly on deep Galilee.

One thing you will notice even before you do a formal scansion of the poem is that the lines have a special rhythm that adds to what is being said. The poem is about the Assyrian's attack on the people of Israel. The rolling rhythm makes the reader think of their advance. Let us now scan the first two lines.

The words that have more than one syllable are *Assyrian, cohorts, gleaming,* and *purple*. The word *Assyrian* has four syllables, but is treated as having three; the second syllable is stressed, while the other two are unstressed. All of the other words have a stress on the first syllable: *cohorts, gleaming, purple*.

When we read the first line aloud, we discover that the words *down, wolf,* and *fold* are stressed. In the second line, none of the other one-syllable words, except *gold*, are stressed.

$$\smile \smile / \smile \smile / \smile \smile / \smile \smile /$$
The Assyrian came down like the wolf on the fold,

$$\smile \smile / \smile \smile / \smile \smile / \smile \smile /$$
And his cohorts were gleaming in purple and gold…

Do you notice the pattern? Byron's poem is written in *anapestic* meter, which has the following pattern: $\smile \smile /$. Notice, too, that the poem has four feet. We would say, then, Byron's poem is in *anapestic tetrameter*.

POETRY & POETICS 16

Exercise 16.1

Scan the following lines and tell whether they are anapestic or not.

1. As he sat on the curb, the American thought about home.   anapestic
2. Did you see that monkey in the cage?   not anapestic
3. Did he dread all the parties that Patty had planned?   anapestic
4. All of us knew that Melissa had parked in the driveway.   not anapestic

Exercise 16.2

Write down the word in the blanks indicated by the description.

1. An iambic line with an imperfect foot has a stressed _____ at the end.
2. A figure of speech in which a word is used in place of another closely associated with it.
3. It is the "measure" of poetry.
4. A _____ is an Old English poet and singer.
5. Two stressed syllables one after another forms a _____ foot.

1. S Y L L A **B** L E
2. M E T O N **Y** M Y
3. M E T E **R**
4. S C **O** P
5. S P O **N** D A I C

Using the letters in the dark boxes above, write down the mystery word and tell what it means.

B Y R O N

Poetry and Poetics 17
Dactylic

There is another three-syllable foot pattern called **dactylic**. Its pattern is reversed: / ᴗ ᴗ . One way that might help you to remember the word *dactylic* is that it comes from the Greek word for "finger," *dactylos*. Look at your fingers. How many joints do you see in each (not counting your thumb)? The answer is three. Also, you will notice that the first joint on your hand is the largest. The first syllable of a dactyl is the "largest," or stressed one.

The American poet Henry Wadsworth Longfellow wrote several beautiful narrative poems using the dactylic stress pattern. The titles of these poems are *Evangeline, The Courtship of Miles Standish,* and *Elizabeth*. They are **narrative poems**, or poems that tell a story. Below are a few lines from *The Courtship of Miles Standish*. It is a very funny, but also serious, poem about the Pilgrims. The following lines describe the captain who protected the Pilgrims from the hostile attacks of the Indians.

Broad in the shoulders, deep-chested, with muscles and sinews of iron;
Brown as a nut was his face, but his russet beard was already
Flaked with patches of snow, as hedges sometimes in November.

Longfellow had copied the rhythm from Greek poetry. Homer's *Iliad* and *Odyssey* are written in dactylic hexameter. Each of the lines has six feet. Many of Longfellow's critics did not like the meter of his narrative poems. They said in so many words that the meter made the poem clumsy. The meter fits Greek poetry, they said, but not English poetry. Readers ignored what the critics said, though. They loved his poems and made Longfellow the most popular poet of his day. It has been said that almost every reading household in America had a copy of the sad but beautiful poem *Evangeline*.

There are other less common stress patterns involving two or three syllables, such as *amphibrach*, which has three syllables with the stress on the second syllable, and *pyrrhic*, which has two syllables, both of them unstressed. However, we will not be going over these stress patterns in detail.

There is also poetry that does not have any regular stress pattern at all; this type of poetry is identified as *free verse*.

Exercise 17.1

Write down the meter of the following words (either anapestic or dactylic). You will notice that some words have a syllable that is stressed slightly, but not as strongly as another. Consider these "in-between" syllables *unstressed*.

1. beautiful   dactylic
2. minuet   anapestic
3. manager   dactylic
4. cardinal   dactylic
5. understand   anapestic
6. organize   dactylic
7. traveling   dactylic
8. terrible   dactylic
9. fingering   dactylic
10. guarantee   anapestic

Exercise 17.2

Write down the stress pattern of the following words (iambic, trochaic, spondaic, anapestic, or dactylic). You will notice that some words have a syllable that is stressed slightly, but not as strongly as another. Consider these "in-between" syllables *unstressed*.

1. Juliet   anapestic
2. barber   trochaic
3. icing   trochaic
4. suitable   dactylic
5. baby   trochaic
6. fistfight   spondaic
7. direct   iambic
8. easy   trochaic
9. single   trochaic
10. violin   anapestic

Poetry and Poetics 18
Stanza Forms and the Ballad

You will remember that a paragraph in poetry is called a *stanza*, which is not separated from other stanzas by an indentation, but rather by a line space. There are six stanzas in Isaac Watts's metrical rendition of Psalm 23. Three of them are presented below. Notice that the break between stanzas is indicated by a space, not by indenting the first line.

> My Shepherd will supply my need,
>   Jehovah is his name;
> In pastures fresh he makes me feed
>   Beside the living stream.
>
> He brings my wandering spirit back,
>   When I forsake his ways;
> And leads me for his mercy's sake,
>   In paths of truth and grace.
>
> When I walk through the shades of death,
>   Thy presence is my stay;
> A word of thy supporting breath
>   Drives all my fears away.

The Ballad

Notice that Isaac Watts' poem is divided into four lines each. A four-lined stanza is called a **quatrain**. This is a very common stanza form that is used especially in **ballads**. Ballads are story poems that are sung. The form of a ballad is very regular and especially suited for singing. The stanza of a ballad is a quatrain with a specific kind of meter. A ballad is iambic with four feet (tetrameter) in lines 1 and 3, and with three feet (trimeter) in lines 2 and 4. Although it is not a ballad, Isaac Watts' hymn is made up of ballad stanzas and meant to be sung. Many other popular hymns sung today are in the ballad stanza form, such John Newton's "Amazing Grace."

Stanzas can be longer or shorter than four lines. These stanzas, too, are given specific names. The most common ones are given below. The names look hard to remember, but again, knowing the meanings of the roots and their related words should help. For instance, a *couple* is two; *triple* means made up of three things; and four *quarters* make up a dollar.

couplet	a stanza made up of two lines
triplet	a stanza made up of three lines
quatrain	a stanza made up of four lines
sestet	a stanza made up of six lines
octave	a stanza made up of eight lines

Exercise 18.1

Memorize the definitions of the terms given above: *couplet, triplet, quatrain, sestet,* and *octave*.

Exercise 18.2

Write down the iambic and trochaic words defined below. Write the scansion marks on the syllables.

Example: To put in order ă r r á n g e

1. A special occasion; something that happens ĕ v é n t

2. A gathering of people celebrating a special occasion
   p á r t y̆

3. A limp rubbery material that is blown up, often seen at birthday celebrations b ă l l ó o n

4. Surprised or shocked ă m á z e d

5. A farmer's fertilizer m ă n ú r e

Poetry and Poetics 19
The Sonnet

One of the most common stanza forms is the **sonnet**. The sonnet is composed of fourteen iambic pentameter lines. Each of the fourteen lines has five feet (pentameter) and has the metrical pattern ⌣ / (iambic).

There are two different kinds of sonnets. One is called an **English sonnet**. The English sonnet is made up of three quatrains (four-line stanzas) and a couplet (a two-line stanza). All together, the quatrains and couplet add up to fourteen lines.

3 quatrains (3 × 4 lines) = **12 lines**
(A quatrain is made up of four lines.)

1 couplet (1 × 2 lines) = **2 lines**
(A couplet is made up of two lines.)

12 lines + 2 lines = **14 lines**
(All sonnets have fourteen lines.)

Some of the best and most famous sonnets written in the English language were those written by William Shakespeare. The English sonnet, then, is sometimes called the **Shakespearean sonnet**.

Another kind of sonnet is called the **Italian sonnet**. It too is composed of fourteen iambic pentameter lines. However, it is made up of an octave (an eight-line stanza) and a sestet (a six-line stanza).

1 octave (1 × 8 lines) = **8 lines**
(A quatrain is made up of four lines.)

1 sestet (1 × 6 lines) = **6 lines**
(A couplet is made up of two lines.)

8 lines + 6 lines = **14 lines**
(All sonnets have fourteen lines.)

The most famous Italian poet of the Middle Ages was Petrarch, who wrote love sonnets. The Italian sonnet, then, also has another name, and that is the **Petrarchan sonnet**.

Exercise 19.1

Be able to answer the following questions orally.

1. What is different between an English sonnet and an Italian sonnet?
2. How many quatrains are there in an English sonnet?
3. Which of the sonnet forms contains a sestet?
4. What are the other names for English sonnet and Italian sonnet?

Exercise 19.2

Choose the correct answer from the choices given.

1. A "paragraph" in poetry is called a _____.
    a) ballad
    b) sonnet
    c) couplet
    d) stanza
    e) English sonnet

2. A stanza made up of iambic quatrains is called a _____.
    a) trochaic stanza
    b) ballad stanza
    c) iambic stanza
    d) Italian sonnet
    e) English sonnet

3. A stanza consisting of eight lines is called a _____.
    a) couplet
    b) triplet
    c) sestet
    d) quatrain
    e) octave

THE SONNET

4. Two lines make up a ____.
   a) a couplet
   b) triplet
   c) sestet
   d) quatrain
   e) octave

5. A line of poetry that has five feet is called ____.
   a) dimeter
   b) trimeter
   c) tetrameter
   d) pentameter
   e) hexameter

Exercise 19.3

Scan the following lines telling its stress pattern and meter. Indicate whether the line is catalectic or acatalectic. The first one has been done for you.

1. / ᴗ / ᴗ / ᴗ / ᴗ /
   Angry, Tom and Bob went far away.
   trochaic tetrameter; catalectic

2. ᴗ / ᴗ / ᴗ / ᴗ / ᴗ /
   The man went out at lunch to buy a tool.   iambic pentameter; acatalectic

3. / /
   Run! Run!   spondaic monometer; acatalectic

4. ᴗ / ᴗ / ᴗ /
   "I'm lost, I'm lost!" she cried.   iambic trimeter; acatalectic

5. / ᴗ ᴗ / ᴗ ᴗ / ᴗ / ᴗ
   Beautiful eagles were flying above us.   dactylic tetrameter; catalectic

Poetry and Poetics 20
Euphony and Perfect Rhyme

Some people think that if a poem doesn't rhyme, it just isn't a poem. That isn't true. One of the greatest poets of all time, John Milton, wrote his opinion about the matter in his introduction to his poem about the fall of Adam and Eve, titled *Paradise Lost*. He said that rhymed poetry was often "jangling." What he meant by that is that poets who rhyme often do not do it with a purpose in mind; they are merely playing with sound. Milton thought that it was not a good thing to use rhyme just for sound effects. His poem *Paradise Lost* did not rhyme. It was written in blank verse. Remember that blank verse is iambic poetry without rhyme.

The excerpt below from William Wordsworth's poem "We are Seven" is a ballad stanza. Like all **traditional ballads**, the poem tells a story—although the writer Wordsworth did not necessarily mean for it to be sung. It tells a story about a little cottage maid who is a asked a simple question: "How many children are in your family?" Her answer confuses and then frustrates the speaker.

> I met a little cottage Girl:
> She was eight years old, she said;
> Her hair was thick with many a curl
> That clustered round her head.

Notice that the poem has four lines. Lines 1 and 3 each have four feet, while lines 2 and 4 each have three feet. Notice also that lines 1 and 3 rhyme, as do lines 2 and 4. When we talk about rhyme in poetry, we are often talking about **end rhyme**. That is to say, the words at the end of the lines rhyme: *girl* rhymes with *curl*, and *said* rhymes with *head*.

What do we mean when we say that two words *rhyme*? Many students have heard about rhyme, but don't know exactly what it is. They know that words that rhyme *sound alike*. But really, this definition is not specific enough. Words can sound alike without being rhyming words. In order for two words to have **perfect rhyme** they have to do the following:

EUPHONY AND PERFECT RHYME

1. Their stressed vowel sounds* must be the same.

2. What comes after the stressed vowel sounds must be the same.

3. What comes before the stressed vowel sounds must be different.

Let us take a look at one of the two end rhymes of Wordsworth's poem, *said* and *head*. Both of these words have the same "short *e*" vowel sound. Notice that they do not have the same spelling. Rhyme does not depend on spelling; it depends on sound. Words that have the same vowel spelling but do not have the same sound are called **eye rhymes**. Eye rhymes are imperfect rhymes. We will be going over imperfect rhymes in the next lesson.

Notice also that the sounds that come after the vowel sounds are also the same. Both words have the consonant sound "d." Finally, the words are different before the vowel sounds. *Head* has the "h" sound, while *said* has the "s" sound.

Exercise 20.1

Write "rhyme" next to the pairs of words that rhyme. If the two words do not rhyme, write "no rhyme." If the two words do not rhyme, but the vowel spellings are the same, write "eye rhyme."

Example 1: math, path	no rhyme
rhyme	
	Example 3: break, leak
Example 2: pin, rim	eye rhyme

6. maid, raid   rhyme

7. night, fight   rhyme

8. could, wood   rhyme

9. our, pour   eye rh.

10. fate, rain   rhyme

11. low, now   eye rh.

---

* Sometimes words have more than one syllable. The stressed vowel is the one used to determine rhyme. To make it simple, however, we will just use *vowel* instead of *stressed vowel*.

12. boot, soot	eye rh.	14. road, goat	no rh.
13. dread, red	rhyme	15. pout, clown	no rh.

Exercise 20.2

You have learned the checklist that tells whether two words rhyme. All of the following words do not rhyme. Write down the number of the rule that explains why the two words do not rhyme. The pair of words may break more than one rule.

Example 1: hair, laid
Rule 2

(The vowel sounds are the same, so rule 1 is not being broken. The sounds before the vowels are different, so rule 3 is not being broken. The sounds after the vowels are not the same—but according to rule 2, they should be. Thus, rule 2 is the answer.)

Example 2: there, their
Rule 3

(The vowel sounds are the same, so rule 1 is not being broken. The sounds that follow the vowels are the same, so rule 2 is not being broken. The sounds before the vowels are not different—but according to rule 2, they should be. Thus, rule 3 is the answer.

1. pale, pail   3
2. Bill, fit   2
3. flip, stop   1
4. mail, maid   2, 3
5. hall, hole   1, 3
6. dear, deer   3
7. meat, mate   1, 3
8. feed, see   2
9. pare, pair   3
10. toil, nail   1

EUPHONY AND PERFECT RHYME

Exercise 20.3

Scan the following pairs of iambic lines and tell the meter of each. The first one has been done for you.

1. We walked along, while bright and red   tetrameter
   Uprose the morning sun.   trimeter

2. And she had made a pipe of straw,   tetrameter
   And music from that pipe could draw.   tetrameter

3. The frosty wind, as if to make amends   pentameter
   For its keen breath, was aiding to our steps.   pentameter

4. I have no name;   dimeter
   I am but two days old.   trimeter

5. The modest Rose puts forth a thorn,   tetrameter
   The humble sheep a threat'ning horn.   tetrameter

Poetry and Poetics 21
Imperfect Rhyme

Assonance and Consonance

As you have already learned, if two words follow the checklist of rules mentioned in the previous lesson, they rhyme. If they obey one but not all of the rules, the rhymes are called **imperfect**. We have already mentioned one kind of imperfect rhyme—**eye rhyme**. Eye rhyme is considered an imperfect rhyme because it does not obey one or more of the rules of rhyme. Remember that rhyme has to do with the *sounds* of words, not their *spelling*. Even though eye rhymes look like rhymes, they are not.

There are other kinds of imperfect rhyme. If two words have the same vowel sounds, but the sounds after the vowels are different, the imperfect rhyme is called **assonance**. The words *page* and *sake*, for example, have assonance. They have the same vowel sound, but the sounds that come after are not the same. If two words rhyme but have *different* vowel sounds, we say that there is **consonance**. The two words *hand* and *lend* have consonance.

So, if rule 2 is not followed, there is assonance. If rule 1 is not followed, there is consonance. What if rule 3 is not obeyed? Rule 3 says that the sounds before a vowel must be different. If they are not different, the words will sound exactly alike. We call this imperfect rhyme **identity**. The words *time* and *thyme* have identity. They are not spelled the same, but the words sound identical. Below is a summary of imperfect rhyme:

Assonance

- Same stressed vowel sounds
- Different sounds after stressed vowels

Consonance

- Different stressed vowel sounds
- Same sounds after stressed vowels

IMPERFECT RHYME

Identity

- Same stressed vowel sounds
- Same sounds before *and* after stressed vowels

Exercise 21.1

Read the following statements. If the statement is false, circle *F*; if the statement is true, circle *T*.

1. (T or **F**) If two words sound like they rhyme but the accented vowels are spelled as if they did not, there is eye rhyme.
2. (T or **F**) Assonance and consonance are both kinds of perfect rhyme.
3. (T or **F**) The words *maid* and *made* have eye rhyme.
4. (**T** or F) The words *riddle* and *paddle* have consonance.
5. (T or **F**) The words *slouch* and *grouch* have identity.

Exercise 21.2

Write down the word in the blanks indicated by the description. The letters in the dark boxes will spell a mystery word.

1. ____ was the poet after whom the English sonnet is named after.
2. ____ was an Italian poet of the Middle Ages.
3. A(n) ____ is an iambic pentameter poem with fourteen lines.
4. A stress pattern with two syllables that is not iambic or spondaic is ____.
5. A line of poetry with six feet is called ____.
6. A line of poetry that has an imperfect ending foot (a foot that is missing a syllable) is called ____.

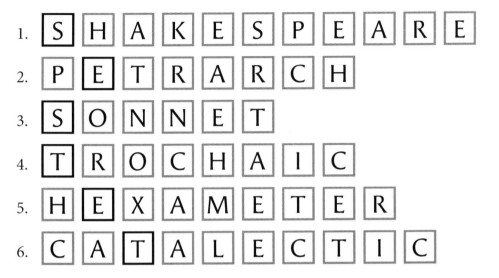

Using the letters in the dark boxes above, write down the mystery word and tell what it means.

Exercise 21.3

> Welcome, red and roundy sun,
> Dropping lowly in the west;
> Now my hard day's work is done,
> I'm as happy as the best.

Which of the following BEST describes the above stanza from John Clare's poem "The Woodcutter's Night Song"?
a) trochaic trimeter acatalectic
b) trochaic tetrameter catalectic
c) iambic dimeter acatalectic
d) dactylic dimeter catalectic
e) anapestic dimeter acatalectic

Poetry and Poetics 22
Alliteration

Words that have the same beginning sounds are given a special name. When two or more words in a line of poetry share beginning sounds, there is said to be **alliteration**. Humorous tongue-twisters often have a lot of alliteration. One such alliterative tongue-twister is "Peter Piper." One version of the tongue-twister is written below.

> If Peter Piper picked a peck of pickled peppers,
> Where's the peck of pickled peppers Peter Piper picked?

Children just love to play with words, and alliteration is one of those things "under the hood" of poetry that they love to tinker with. The most obvious reason poets use rhyme and alliteration is for *euphony*, or to make a pleasing sound for the listener. People, especially children, like to listen to the sounds of words, and rhyme and alliteration can play an important part in creating that pleasure. But there is much more to rhyme and alliteration than just the sounds of words. What more could there be? Why do poets rhyme and use alliteration other than to play with sounds?

There are so many other purposes to rhyme or alliteration. It is not just to make a poem sound beautiful. Take for instance, Longfellow's use of alliteration in his poem *The Courtship of Miles Standish*. The excerpt below is taken from a part of the poem in which a native has entered the council chamber of the Pilgrims and has brought a message of war from his chief in the form of a snake filled with arrows. At the council meeting is the fearless Miles Standish, who responds to this hostile message with hot fury. He jerks the arrows out of the skin and replaces them with gunpowder. Message in hand, the native returns home through the woods:

> Silently out of the room then glided the glistening savage,
> Bearing the serpent's skin, and seeming himself like a serpent,
> Winding his sinuous way in the dark to the depths of the forest.

Notice the alliteration in the poem. *Silently, savage, serpent's, skin, seeming, serpent,* and *sinuous* are all words that begin with the letter *s*. There is also a different kind of consonance with the words *glistening, depths,* and *forest,* all of which have the *s* sound in them. The poet is trying to imitate the sound of a snake to give us an image of the messenger who is snake-like in his trickiness. Longfellow's purpose in using alliteration, then, is to create an image in the reader's head.

Exercise 22.1

Tell whether the words have perfect rhyme or imperfect rhyme. If there is imperfect rhyme, identify it as consonance, assonance, or identity.

1. rain, sane   perfect
2. rich, stitch   perfect
3. dark, Bart   assonance
4. rode, road   identity
5. bat, bit   consonance
6. pet, red   assonance
7. pawn, dawn   perfect
8. like, bite   assonance
9. tarp, harp   perfect
10. tear, tare   consonance

Exercise 22.2

Write down the stress pattern of the following words as iambic, trochaic, spondaic, anapestic, or dactylic. You will notice that some words have a syllable that is stressed slightly, but not as strongly as another. Consider these "in-between" syllables *unstressed*.

1. telescope   dactylic
2. absolute   anapestic
3. alone   iambic
4. indirect   anapestic
5. snakeskin   spondaic
6. oxen   trochaic
7. surprise   iambic
8. Englishman   dactylic
9. cardboard   spondaic
10. eyeglass   spondaic

ALLITERATION

Exercise 22.3

> Sing a song of seasons!
> Something bright in all!
> Flowers in the summer,
> Fires in the fall!

Which of the following BEST describes the stress, meter and euphony of the above stanza?
a) iambic pentameter with alliteration in line 1
b) dactylic dimeter with alliteration in line 1
c) trochaic trimeter with lines 2 and 4 catalectic
d) trochaic tetrameter with lines 1 and 3 catalectic
e) iambic tetrameter with spondaic dimeter in line 4

Poetry and Poetics 23
Masculine and Feminine Rhyme

So far we have gone over rhyming words of only one syllable. We are now going to talk about rhyming words of two or more syllables. The same three rules that you learned in a previous lesson apply to words of two or more syllables.

Is it harder to rhyme words of more than one syllable? There are two answers to that question. Yes and no. Finding a rhyming word for two- or three-syllable words can be just as easier finding a rhyming word for a one-syllable word—as long as the accent is on the last syllable. Let's take the word *parade*, for instance. This word has a stress on the last syllable. Just as many words rhyme with *parade* as the one-syllable made because we don't have to take into account what comes before the stressed vowel. Remember, in rhyme, what comes *before* the stressed vowel must be different. So, in the word *parade*, we must concern ourselves with only the stressed vowel *a* and the sounds after it.

It's harder, however, with two- or three-syllable words whose stress is not at the end. Let's take the word *beautiful* as an example. It would be more than a challenge to find a word that rhymes with *beautiful*. In fact, it would be impossible. This word has three syllables and the stress is on first syllable. That means that all the sounds following the stressed vowel (the "long *u*" sound) must be the same. There are no words that rhyme with the word *beautiful*.

We have a special term to describe rhyming words that have a stress on the last syllable. We call the rhyme **masculine rhyme**. Rhyming words such as *bright* and *polite* are masculine rhymes. When two words that have a stress on a syllable other than the last, we call it **feminine rhyme**. William Wordsworth often used this more unusual rhyme in his poetry. In the following excerpt, Wordsworth rhymes the word *pottage* with *cottage*. The rhyme is feminine rhyme.

MASCULINE AND FEMININE RHYME

> By the same fire to boil their pottage,
> Two poor old dames as I have known,
> Will often live in one small cottage,
> But she, poor woman, dwelt alone.

Feminine rhymes not only are more unusual but also can be more interesting, as in the following from William Wordsworth's "The Sun Has Long Been Set." Notice the two pairs of feminine rhymes, *parading/masquerading* and *blisses/this is*.

> Who would go "parading"
> In London, "and masquerading,"
> On such a night of June
> With that beautiful soft half-moon,
> And all these innocent blisses?
> On such a night as this is!

Exercise 23.1

Identify the rhymes in the following words as perfect rhyme, assonance, consonance, eye rhyme, or identity. If it is a perfect rhyme, tell whether the rhyme is masculine or feminine.

1. boat, float   perfect
2. judge, fudge   perfect
3. follows, bellows   consonance
4. planted, ranted   perfect
5. less, dress   perfect
6. street, mean   assonance
7. whales, Wales   identity
8. Paris, Harris   perfect
9. wood, stood   perfect
10. plaid, raid   consonance

POETRY & POETICS 23

Exercise 23.2

Write down the word in the blanks indicated by the description. The letters in the dark boxes will spell a mystery word.

1. An iambic foot has a ____ on the second syllable.
2. A three-syllable stress pattern that has a stress on the third syllable is called ____.
3. The poet ____ wrote "The Destruction of Sennacherib."
4. The poet ____ wrote *Evangeline*.
5. A three-syllable stress pattern that has a stress on the first syllable is called ____.
6. A line of iambs that ends with a stressed syllable must be ____.
7. The poet ____ wrote "The Barefoot Boy."

1. S T R E S S
2. A N A P E S T I C
3. B Y R O N
4. L O N G F E L L O W
5. D A C T Y L I C
6. A C A T A L E C T I C
7. W H I T T I E R

Using the letters in the dark boxes above, write down the mystery word and tell what it means.

S P O N D E E

MASCULINE AND FEMININE RHYME

Exercise 23.3

> Little drops of water,
> Little grains of sand,
> Make the mighty ocean
> And the pleasant land.
>
> Thus the little minutes,
> Humble though they be,
> Make the mighty ages
> Of eternity.

Which of the following BEST describes the stress, meter, and euphony of the poem "Little Things" by Ebenezer Cobham Brewer, printed above?

a) anapestic trimeter catalectic with end rhyme in lines 2 and 4
b) dactylic dimeter with alliteration in line 3
c) trochaic trimeter that is catalectic and contains end rhyme in lines 2 and 4
d) iambic trimeter with alliteration in line 3
e) iambic trimeter with end rhyme in lines 1 and 3

Poetry and Poetics 24
Internal Rhyme and Caesura

So far we have talked about end rhyme. Poets also use internal rhyme, or rhyme within a line of poetry. Let us look at an illustration from William Wordsworth's poem "The Idiot Boy."

> Poor Susan moans, poor Susan groans.

Here the word *moans* rhymes with the word *groans*. Because the words do not fall at the end of two lines, their rhyme is called *internal rhyme*. Notice that there is a pause in the middle of the line, too. Partly made by the rhyme, this break or pause in the line is called a **caesura** (*seh-zhoor-a*). Like rhyme, poets can use caesura in ways to communicate their meaning more effectively.

Rhyming dictionaries have been published to help poets in their craft. One of the most famous rhyming dictionaries was published by Clement Wood in 1936. It is important to understand how to use the dictionary, however. It is arranged according to what syllable of the word is receiving the stress and according to the vowel sound.

If a student doesn't have a rhyming dictionary handy, however, he can make his own. It merely involves going through the alphabet of sounds. If you want to find a word that rhymes with the word *fate*, for example, go through the alphabet for words: *ate, bait, Kate, date, fate, gate,* etc. (You see that there is no word spelled Cate, but there is a word with the "hard *c*" sound, spelled *Kate*.) You also need to go through the two- and three-sound rhymes for words such as *crate* and *straight*. Feminine rhymes, we have said, can get more complicated. It is easier, however, to use a rhyming dictionary. But it is easiest to use a computer program. There are now rhyming programs that have made the poet's craft an easy job (as far as finding rhymes). You need only enter the word that you want to use, and it will provide all the possible rhymes to the word.

INTERNAL RHYME AND CAESURA

Exercise 24.1

Draw a double vertical line (||) marking the caesura in the following lines of poetry. The first one has been done for you. If a line has no caesura, write "NC."

1. When with her load || she turned about

2. Ill fed she was, || and thinly clad

3. Oh! what's the matter? || what's the matter?

4. Once upon a midnight dreary, || while I pondered, weak and weary

5. But when the ice our streams did fetter   NC

6. It caught his eye, || he saw it plain

7. His little hands, || when flowers were seen

8. And I'll be true for Patty's sake   NC
   And she'll be true for mine.   NC

9. Startled at the stillness broken || by reply so aptly spoken

10. Then I was certain I had never meant
    To let him have them. || Never show surprise!

Exercise 24.2

Twilight it is, and the far woods are dim, and the rooks cry and call.
Down in the valley the lamps, and the mist, and a star over all,
There by the rick, where they thresh, is the drone at an end,
Twilight it is, and I travel the road with my friend.

I think of the friends who are dead, who were dear long ago in the past,
Beautiful friends who are dead, though I know that death cannot last;
Friends with the beautiful eyes that the dust has defiled,
Beautiful souls who were gentle when I was a child.

Which of the following BEST describes the poem "Twilight" by John Masefield, printed above?
(a)) dactylic hexameter in rhyming couplets

b) anapestic hexameter with alliteration in the fourth line of the first stanza

c) iambic hexameter with alliteration in the fourth line of the first stanza

d) trochaic hexameter with alliteration in the fourth line of the first stanza

e) anapestic heptameter with alliteration in the first line of the second stanza

Exercise 24.3

Write down the word in the blanks indicated by the description.

1. An ____ foot has the metrical pattern ⌣ ⌣ /.

2. A break in the line of poetry is called a ____.

3. Words that sound alike may be said to ____.

4. Letters added to the end of a word to change its meaning or form are called a ____.

5. ____ is a word meaning "little lamb."

6. ____ is a word referring to a little bird.

1. A N A P E S T I C
2. C A E S U R A
3. R H Y M E
4. S U F F I X
5. L A M B K I N
6. N E S T L I N G

Using the letters in the dark boxes above, write down the mystery word and tell what it means.

C H I L L

Poetry and Poetics 25
Rhyme Schemes

We have already talked about certain stanza forms. These stanza forms all have a particular rhyme scheme. For example, a ballad often has an *abab* rhyme scheme. A rhyme scheme is a pattern of rhyme. The rhyme scheme *abab* merely means that lines 1 and 3 rhyme, as do lines 2 and 4. We call the end word of the first line and all other end words that rhyme with it *a*. The first end word that does not rhyme with the word we call *b*, and so on. In the following ballad stanza by William Wordsworth, the word pairs that rhyme are *maid/said* and *be/me*. Note that *maid / said* is an imperfect rhyme, more specifically an eye rhyme.

"Sisters and brothers, little maid,	*a*
How many may you be?"	*b*
"How many? seven in all," she said,	*a*
And wondering looked at me.	*b*

The English and Italian sonnets are different in their rhyme schemes. The English sonnet's rhyme scheme is *abab cdcd efef gg*, while the Italian sonnet's rhyme scheme is *abba abba cde cde*. The first poem below is a student example of an English sonnet. Note that *Word/work* is not a perfect rhyme, but rather assonance. The second example is of an Italian sonnet titled "On the Grasshopper and Cricket"; it was written by John Keats, who lived around the time of William Wordsworth.

An English Sonnet

"Let me tell you what I like about spring,"	*a*
Said the big-bellied robin to his friend.	*b*
"I like spring because I can eat and sing,	*a*
Eat and sing till the summer's end."	*b*
"That's good for you, perhaps," said Big Red Ant,	*c*
"But some of us must work to live and eat.	*d*
I can't afford to sing in spring, I can't.	*c*
I build, I forage, and the day's complete."	*d*

A lad, who had heard these two on his way, said:	*e*
"God has taught me a lesson in his Word,	*f*
That we must work to get our daily bread;	*e*
And give God our thanks for our daily work.	*f*
For neither sloth nor work can give us meat:	*g*
By God's hands our hands bear fruit, and food to eat."	*g*

An Italian Sonnet

The poetry of earth is never dead:	*a*
When all the birds are faint with the hot sun,	*b*
And hide in cooling trees, a voice will run	*b*
From hedge to hedge about the new-mown mead;	*a*
That is the Grasshopper's—he takes the lead	*a*
In summer luxury—he has never done	*b*
With his delights; for when tired out with fun	*b*
He rests at ease beneath some pleasant weed.	*a*
The poetry of earth is ceasing never:	*c*
On a lone winter evening, when the frost	*d*
Has wrought a silence, from the stove there shrills	*e*
The Cricket's song, in warmth increasing ever,	*c*
And seems to one in drowsiness half lost,	*d*
The Grasshopper's among some grassy hills.	*e*

Exercise 25.1

Choose the correct answer from the choices given.

1. Which of the following is NOT true about rhyme?
    a) There are more masculine than feminine rhymes in poetry.
    b) John Milton said that poems do not have to rhyme.
    c) A feminine rhyme ends in an unstressed syllable.
    d) A masculine rhyme can be made with two words that are iambic.
    e) In rhyme, the unstressed vowels must be the same.

2. Which of the following is true of the two words *lament* and *lenient*?
   a) They are perfect rhymes.
   b) They do not have consonance.
   c) They have assonance.
   (d) They have alliteration.
   e) They are masculine rhymes.

3. What poem has fourteen lines with an ending couplet?
   a) a ballad
   (b) an English sonnet
   c) a quatrain
   d) an Italian sonnet
   e) a triplet

4. What did the poet Milton say about rhyme?
   a) Rhyme should not be used in any poetry.
   b) Rhyme was not beautiful.
   c) Rhyme does not have to serve a purpose.
   d) Poems can rhyme but do not have to.
   e) The best poetry rhymes.

5. Which of the following means a break in a line of poetry?
   a) caesura
   b) sonnet
   c) English Sonnet
   d) internal rhyme
   e) hexameter

Exercise 25.2

Write "S" next to the words that are spondaic and "D" next to the words that are dactylic. There will be one spondaic and one dactylic in each word list.

1. a) paper
   b) greatness
   c) forsaken
   d) ministry   D
   e) pillbox   S

2. a) radio   D
   b) toenail   S
   c) Billy
   d) recalling
   e) apply

3. a) attire
   b) french fries   S
   c) vitamin   D
   d) spaghetti
   e) signal

4. a) yo-yo   S
   b) butter
   c) identity
   d) people
   e) loneliness   D

5. a) knowledge
   b) pastor
   c) playground   S
   d) minuscule   D
   e) fortify

Exercise 25.3

After reviewing the previous lessons, scan the following the lines and write down the stress and meter.

Example: He knows my name.
iambic dimeter

1. I lost the game.   iambic dimeter
2. Adults and children go.   iambic trimeter
3. I see and know.   iambic dimeter
4. Pickles, pears, and apples.   trochaic trimeter
5. Tonight I'll eat my meal in silence, Tom.   iambic tetrameter

Poetry and Poetics 26
Writing Music to Poetry

In the past, it was very common for hymnbooks to contain words without music. In some of these books, the names of suggested tunes would be given, such as Duke Street, St. Thomas, St. Anne's, or Bangor. People would learn these tunes by listening to the leader and remembering them from repeated singing. The tunes can be sung to a number of the hymns printed in the book, according to the specific meter of the hymn. For example, the tune Duke Street can be sung to hymns made up of four iambic tetrameter lines. Such a meter is called long meter (abbreviated L.M.). One of the oldest and best known tunes, Old Hundred, fits this pattern. The tune, which first appeared in the French Genevan Psalter in 1551, is called Old Hundred because it is often sung to a metrical rendition of Psalm 100.

The tune St. Thomas can be sung to hymns made up of four lines, in which the first, second, and fourth are iambic trimeter and the third is iambic tetrameter. The meter is called short meter (abbreviated S.M.).

The tune St. Anne's, which is sung to Isaac Watts' hymn "O God, Our Help in Ages Past," is in common meter. Common meter (abbreviated C.M.) has the same rhythmical pattern as the ballad stanza: the first and third lines are iambic tetrameter, while the second and fourth lines are iambic trimeter. "God Moves in a Mysterious Way," written by the eighteenth-century poet William Cowper, was written in common meter; "Amazing Grace," written by Cowper's friend and spiritual mentor John Newton, is also in common meter; it is one of the best known hymns of all time. Hymns can be written in other meters as well, but common meter, short meter and long meter are the most common. Not only hymns, but also many popular songs can be sung to these meters and tunes.

Exercise 26.1

Be able to answer the following questions orally.

1. What are the three most common meters in Christian hymnody?

2. What are their respective stress patterns?

3. What is Old Hundred and why is it called such?

4. Give an example of a hymn in common meter.

Exercise 26.2

Research the tunes St. Thomas, St. Anne's, Duke Street, and Bangor, and discover what they sound like. As an optional assignment, you may compose words to fit one of them.

WRITING MUSIC TO POETRY

Exercise 26.3

> Twinkle, twinkle, little star!
> How I wonder what you are,
> Up above the world so high,
> Like a diamond in the sky.
>
> When the glorious sun is set,
> When the grass with dew is wet,
> Then you show your little light,
> Twinkle, twinkle all the night.
>
> In the dark-blue sky you keep,
> And often through my curtains peep,
> For you never shut your eye,
> Till the sun is in the sky.
>
> As your bright and tiny spark
> Guides the traveller in the dark,
> Though I know not what you are,
> Twinkle, twinkle, little star!

Which of the following BEST describes the children's verse "Twinkle, Twinkle, Little Star," printed above?
a) iambic tetrameter acatalectic
b) iambic tetrameter catalectic
c) iambic trimeter with rhyme scheme *aabb*
d) trochaic trimeter with rhyme scheme *aabb*
e) trochaic tetrameter catalectic

Poetry and Poetics 27
Narrative Poetry

Do you like listening to stories? Most likely your answer is *yes*. Who doesn't like a story! It is not surprising that some of the best beloved classics are stories and poems in one—a double treat, you might say. Called narrative poems, these works contain elements of both poetry—such as meter, interesting language, and sometimes rhyme—as well as elements of storytelling—such as character development, plot, irony and climax. America's most beloved poet of the 1800s, Henry Wadsworth Longfellow (1807–1882) wrote several narrative poems that became instant "hits"—*Evangeline*, *The Courtship of Miles Standish*, and *Hiawatha*. Like traditional ballads, these poems all tell stories. But unlike ballads, they were not written in the ballad stanza (alternating tetrameter and trimeter) and were not originally songs. (*Evangeline* and the *Courtship of Miles Standish* were written in dactylic hexameter and *Hiawatha* in trochaic tetrameter.) These narrative poems were popular not only in America, but also in England, where Longfellow was given at his death the special honor of having a memorial placed in his name in Poet's Corner of Westminster Abbey, the same place where Geoffrey Chaucer (c. 1340–1400) and other great poets are buried or memorialized. Longfellow was the first American to be given such an honor.

Another narrative poem that instantly received wide and wild acclaim when it was written is *Idylls of the King*, written by Alfred Tennyson (1809–1892). The work is actually a collection of separate tales written in iambic pentameter about the legendary King Arthur. Arguably one of the best narrative poems ever written in the English language, *Idylls of the King* contains adventures of the Round Table knights and of its king and his eventual tragic death.

Idylls of the King is excellent on many levels. First, it is excellent as a story. Like a good adventure story, it has action and suspense. There are short story or dramatic elements, such as mistaken identity in addition to pathetic death scenes that one more ordinarily finds in tragic plays like *King Lear*, *Hamlet* or the ancient Greek tragedies. The work is also excellent as a poem. Tennyson's meter and choice of words help to make the stories more lush, expressive, powerful and full of pathos.

Another reason why *Idylls of the King* is a highly respected classic is that the stories' themes are stirring—themes of loyalty and betrayal, of youth and age, and of faith and faithlessness. In the poem, Tennyson was able to express the mind of his own country and age, when people living in the Western world were beginning to seriously question their faith. Tennyson records the thoughts and feelings that came to English people toward the end of the 1800s as they watched the decline and decay of the great British Empire.

For Christians, *Idylls of the King* holds special meaning, as Arthur, betrayed by one of his knights, is a Christ figure in the story. A Christ figure is a characterization of the sufferings, ministry or death of Christ in a literary character. Christians believe that the Old Testament characters Joseph, Boaz, David, Moses, Jonah and Joshua are all christ figures, or more appropriately, types. Types are different from Christ figures in that usually the meaning of the word *type* is restricted to the Old Testament foreshadowings of Christ. The Gospel of Matthew, for example, records Jesus as saying, "As Jonah was three days and three nights in the whale's belly, so shall the Son of man be three days and three nights in the heart of the earth." Christians say, then, that Jonah, is a type of Christ in that he suffered three days and nights in the dark belly of the whale before he was spewed out upon the shore as Christ suffered the pangs of death and punishment of God for three days and nights after his crucifixion and before his resurrection. Other famous English and American novels and short stories use Christ figures, such as *Old Man and the Sea* by Ernest Hemingway (1899–1961), which won great literary prizes.

Matthew 12:40

Alfred Tennyson also wrote a very well-received narrative poem titled *Enoch Arden*. Like Enoch of the Old Testament, mentioned in Genesis 5, the main character of the story, Enoch Arden, disappears and

POETRY & POETICS 27

dies in a shipwreck—well, he dies but *doesn't* die. If this contradiction intrigues you, look forward to reading the poem when you are a little older. In addition to its wonderful poetry, *Enoch Arden* contains many elements usually associated with stories and drama, such as foreshadowing, dramatic irony, and situational irony. When a story writer or poet uses foreshadowing, he is giving an "appetizer," or taste, of what is to come later in the story. There are many things hinted about Enoch Arden in the beginning of the poem that come to pass, For example, in the beginning of the poem Enoch as a child is playing among the flotsam, or ship wreckage with Annie, his future wife. This scene would be called a foreshadowing, as Enoch later is shipwrecked later in the poem. For a discussion of situational irony and dramatic irony, see the section on "Lyman Dean's Testimonials."

Other great narrative poems include Wordsworth's *Michael*, which is a tragedy that showed the disastrous effects of the Industrial Revolution, and Geoffrey Chaucer's *Canterbury Tales,* which is a collection of tales told by pilgrims on their way to the shrine of Thomas Beckett in Canterbury. Perhaps one major reason why these poems have endured is that they are great not only as poetry, but also as stories. There is, however, really too much to say about these two great narrative poems to describe them in full detail here.

Exercise 27.1

Be able to answer the following questions orally.

1. What story elements are often contained in narrative poetry? What poetic elements?

2. How is narrative poetry different from the traditional ballad?

3. Name some narrative that poems were widely praised when they first were published. What century were they written?

4. What story elements does *Idylls of the King* have that help make it great?

Exercise 27.2

Be able to identify the following terms:

- foreshadowing
- dramatic irony
- situational irony
- Christ figure
- type

Exercise 27.3

Stand! the ground's your own, my braves!
Will ye give it up to slaves?
Will ye look for greener graves?
Hope ye mercy still?
What's the mercy despots feel?
Hear it in that battle-peal!
Read it on yon bristling steel!
Ask it—ye who will.

Fear ye foes who kill for hire?
Will ye to your homes retire?
Look behind you! they're afire!
And, before you, see
Who have done it!—From the vale
On they come!—And will ye quail?—
Leaden rain and iron hail
Let their welcome be!

In the God of battles trust!
Die we may—and die we must;
But, O, where can dust to dust
Be consigned so well,
As where Heaven its dews shall shed
On the martyred patriot's bed,
And the rocks shall raise their head,
Of his deeds to tell!

Which of the following BEST describes the poem "Warren's Address to the American Soldiers" by John Pierpont, printed above?
a) iambic tetrameter in the first four lines of each stanza and iambic trimeter in the last four lines of each stanza
b) trochaic tetrameter catalectic in lines 1, 2, 3, 5, 6 and 7 of each stanza and trochaic trimeter catalectic in lines 4 and 8
c) iambic tetrameter catalectic throughout
d) dactylic trimeter with rhyme scheme *aaabcccb*
e) anapestic trimeter with rhyme scheme *aaabaaab*

Poetry and Poetics 28
Epic Poems

It is always interesting to hear and read about the firsts of things—the first European to come to America, the first airplane flight, the first computer. If you do not know these "firsts," you will be disappointed because airplanes, computers and explorers do not directly concern poetry and you will have to find out these facts on your own. In this section, however, you *will* learn about the first known poem and epic and who wrote it. You also learn about the first *English* epic. But first, you need to know just what an epic is.

An epic is a kind of narrative poem, as it tells a story. The Ancient Greek philosopher Plato maintained that epics differed from narrative poems in that epics were dramatic. However, in the previous section you learned that such a claim is not true—at least judging from English literature. *Enoch Arden* and other narrative poems are clearly dramatic, like epics, but we would never call *Enoch Arden* or *Evangeline* epics. An epic is different from a narrative poem in that contains a larger-than-life hero that has an adventure.

War and sea journeys are certainly adventurous, and that is what concerns the *Iliad* and *Odyssey*, the first known epics and poems written in the Western world. When the Trojan prince Paris kidnaps Helen, beautiful Queen of Sparta, the Greek kings, including Odysseus, unite and embark for Troy to get her back. When they do, the ugly war between Greece and Troy begins. What happens during the war is told in the *Iliad*. What happens after the war, mostly concerning Odysseus' ten-year-long voyage home, is the subject of the *Odyssey*.

There are several heroes in the *Iliad*. One is Achilles, who is certainly larger than life in that he was, as the son of the sea nymph Thetis, a god. Achilles could not be killed, an excellent thing to boast of in war. Who would want to fight a foe that could not be killed? However, he did have *one* hard-to-get-to, vulnerable spot—his heel. And not surprisingly, an arrow in the course of the war, shot by the Trojan prince Paris, happens to lodge there.

Odysseus is a hero in both the *Iliad* and the *Odyssey*. In the *Odyssey*, Odysseus goes on an adventure (his journey home) and on the way meets up a one-eyed cannibalistic Cyclops, sirens who enchant sailors to their destruction, the Lotus Eaters whose diet makes them idle, and with the cattle of Helios, which the crew of Odysseus eats to their own peril. Each of the adventures shows Odysseus cleverness and strength.

When Odysseus returns home from his ten-year voyage home, his adventures do not stop. While he was away at war and on his journey home, men have been pestering his wife, eating from his larder and threatening to kill his only son Telemachus. In one of the most dramatic scenes in literature, Odysseus, disguised as a beggar, shows up at a feast where these men are making their boasts and talking about Odysseus who was, so they thought, lost forever in the war or at sea. At the feast a contest takes place, which involves hitting a target with a bow—Odysseus' bow, which requires a strength to pull that only Odysseus has. The men badger the "beggar" for showing up at the feast, and mock him for trying to do what they themselves could not. The "beggar" then reveals himself by stringing his bow and "taking care of business."

There are few true epics in the English language. The earliest was written in Old English, titled *Beowulf*. It deals with a hero (named Beowulf) who shows his heroic qualities by great feats, such as swimming in the sea while fighting sea monsters, wielding a giant's sword, and encountering three monsters: Grendel, Grendel's mother and a dragon. Grendel is an ugly giant—a swamp "thing" that makes attacks upon the Danish mead hall, where warriors meet, stories are told and treasure distributed. One of the most exciting moments of the epic occurs when Grendel enters the hall and begins his senseless and chaotic ravaging. He then reaches for Beowulf, whose grip takes the monster by surprise. Never before has he experienced anything like it. He tries to retreat, but in one act of heroic bravery and superhuman strength, Beowulf rips off the monster's arm and saves the Danish kingdom from destruction.

EPIC POEMS

The most respected epic written in the English language is John Milton's *Paradise Lost*. The problem with this epic is that it is difficult to say who the larger-than-life hero is. Some readers in the past have said that it is actually the angelic rebel Satan. It is Satan, in fact, who has the adventure, including flying out of the confines of hell and traveling to Earth where he deceives Eve. Milton may have identified with rebels, as he himself was one. He fought against the king—if not with a sword, with words. He worked in the government of Oliver Cromwell, who made war against the king and became England's leader after the king's beheading. But as a Christian poet, Milton would not have tried to praise the devil's work. In fact, the purpose of his poem is stated from the very beginning of the poem. He wanted to "justify the ways of God to Man." If the reader feels sorry for Satan's hopeless condition in the beginning of the poem, Satan's later actions and dialogue make it clear that such sympathy is wrong. It's almost as if the poet tried first to stir up the reader's sympathy only to destroy it by presenting the devil's distorted ways of thinking. If Satan, then, is the main character or hero of the epic, he is more properly identified as an antihero, which is a hero without the normal positive qualities of a hero, such as bravery and self-sacrifice.

Exercise 28.1

Be able to answer the following questions orally.

1. What is an epic? Give one example of an epic written in Ancient Greek and one example in English.

2. How did the ancient philosopher Plato distinguish epics from other narrative poems?

3. What is the main action of the *Iliad*? Of the *Odyssey*?

4. How are both Odysseus and Beowulf typical heroes?

5. Why do some readers think that Satan is a hero of John Milton's *Paradise Lost*? How is Satan not a typical hero?

Exercise 28.2

After reviewing the previous lessons, scan the following the lines and write down the stress and meter.

Example: He knows my̆ name. (˘ / ˘ /)
iambic dimeter

1. Understanding my problem and giving advice.   anapestic tetrameter
2. Simple and easy for Jacquelyn.   dactylic trimeter
3. Bob: watch, wait, guard.   spondaic dimeter
4. Buttery casserole.   dactylic dimeter
5. While I was waiting for lunch to be served by Elizabeth.   dactylic trimeter

Exercise 28.3

> When you are old and gray and full of sleep,
> And nodding by the fire, take down this book,
> And slowly read, and dream of the soft look
> Your eyes had once, and of their shadows deep.

Which of the following BEST describes the stanza taken from "When You Are Old" by W. B. Yeats, printed above?

a) iambic tetrameter with a caesura between "fire" and "take" in line 2
b) trochaic pentameter
c) iambic pentameter
d) anapestic tetrameter
e) dactylic trimeter

Poetry and Poetics 29
Lyric Poetry

A *lyric* is a personal poem. Unlike a narrative poem or an epic which focuses on plot, lyrical poetry deals with the inner feelings of the poet. Lyric poetry is generally shorter than either epics or narrative poems, but that doesn't mean that it can be read quickly. Lyric poetry can be dense with meaning and requires slow reading, or at least multiple readings, if the reader is to understand and appreciate most of what the poet is trying to say.

Lyric poetry includes elegies, which are funeral poems and odes, which are poems that deal with serious topics. Some of the most famous odes in the English language were written by John Keats (1795–1821). Surprisingly, these great works were all written in a short period right before Keats' untimely death at the age of twenty-five from tuberculosis. The odes deal with the serious topics of art and death in such a striking way, that they have become some of the most praised, quoted and talked about odes in English literature.

One of Keats' odes is titled "Ode to a Grecian Urn." The ode deals with the thoughts that John Keats had on an urn from ancient Greece, made so long, long ago. An ancient artist had pictured, among other things, musicians playing. Although he could not hear the music—the musicians had died thousands of years ago and it was only a picture—Keats could hear a more "endearing" or special music. What was it? It is the eternal song that lives through the ages—the beauty of art and poetry. In the poem, then, Keats talks about death, beauty and art. Keats' other odes include "Ode on Melancholy," "Ode to a Nightingale," "Ode on Indolence," "To Autumn," and "Ode to Psyche." In the odes, Keats uses *apostrophe*. In other words, the speaker of the odes addresses or talks to things in a figure of speech, such as the pictures on the Grecian Urn and the Nightingale.

Exercise 29.1

Be able to answer the following questions orally.

1. What is a lyric poem and how is it different from narrative poetry?
2. What is an elegy?
3. What is an ode?
4. Name several famous odes written by John Keats. What are they about?

Exercise 29.2

Write one rhyme for each of the following words.

1. time
2. fat
3. hut
4. name
5. pole
6. chew
7. pool
8. waste
9. birch
10. bruise

Exercise 29.3

> My country, 'tis of thee,
> Sweet land of liberty,
> Of thee I sing;
> Land where my fathers died,
> Land of the Pilgrims' pride;
> From every mountain side,
> Let freedom ring.
>
> My native country, thee—
> Land of the noble free—
> Thy name I love;
> I love thy rocks and rills,

LYRIC POETRY

Thy woods and templed hills;
My heart with rapture thrills,
Like that above.

Let music swell the breeze,
And ring from all the trees
Sweet freedom's song;
Let mortal tongues awake;
Let all that breathe partake;
Let rocks their silence break—
The sound prolong.

Our fathers' God, to Thee,
Author of liberty,
To Thee we sing:
Long may our land be bright
With freedom's holy light:
Protect us by Thy might,
Great God, our King.

Which of the following BEST describes the patriotic poem "America" by Samuel Francis Smith, printed above?

a) a four-stanza iambic trimeter and dimeter poem with an apostrophe to America
b) a four-stanza trochaic trimeter and dimeter ode
c) a four-stanza iambic tetrameter and dimeter epic with the rhyme scheme *aabcccb*
d) a four-stanza iambic pentameter narrative poem with the rhyme scheme *aabccca*
e) a five-stanza lyric with the rhyme scheme *aaacccc*

Poetry and Poetics 30
Themes and Topics of Poetry

When you meet with your friends, what do you talk about? Baseball? Books? A vacation that you took last summer? These are all typical topics of conversation for young people (and adults as well). Poets, too, have subjects that they like to talk about.

One topic that appears frequently in poetry is the idea that life passes by quickly and that we must make the best use of our time—*seize the day*, in other words. The Latin expression is *carpe diem*, which originally appeared in a poem written by the poet Horace (65–8 BC). Perhaps the most familiar English poem that has this theme of *carpe diem* is "To the Virgins, To Make Much of Time," written by Robert Herrick (1591–1674). The first of the four stanzas of this poem is printed below.

> Gather ye rose-buds while ye may:
>   Old Time is still a-flying;
> And this same flower that smiles today,
>   Tomorrow will be dying.

Another common topic of poetry is love. Throughout the ages—in ancient Greece and Rome as well as throughout the history of English literature—this strong emotion has inspired poets to write. In fact, the Sonnet—a form of poetry which you learned in an earlier section—is typically a *love* poem. The Medieval Italian poet Petrarch wrote many sonnets that deal with love. William Shakespeare wrote more than 150 sonnets, many of which deal with love (as well as those with the theme of *carpe diem*). In the Victorian Period, the poet Elizabeth Barrett Browning (1806–1861) wrote love poetry to her husband, the poet Robert Browning, in a book of sonnets titled *Sonnets from the Portuguese*.

Another popular topic of poetry is death. The deep sorrow that comes after a close friend or relative dies has inspired such poets as Alfred Tennyson (1809–1892) who wrote one of his most respected poems *In Memoriam* after his friend Arthur Hallam died. John Donne (1572–1631) wrote a very famous poem about death titled "Death Be Not Proud," in which he talks about man's victory over death in the resurrection. Donne himself had been very close to death before having written the poem.

Another topic that has seemed to inspire great poets is spiritual or religious devotion. Some of the best-known poets were religious men. One of the greatest poet of the 1500s, John Donne, was an Anglican priest, as was his contemporary George Herbert (1593–1633). These two poets are arguably the best metaphysical poets, a group of writers that also includes Andrew Marvell (1621–1678), Robert Herrick (1591–1674), and Henry Vaughn (1622–1695). The word *metaphysical* is very similar in meaning to the word *spiritual*. The famous dictionary writer Samuel Johnson applied the term to this group of writers because they wrote about spiritual things. One famous poem, written by John Donne, is his Sonnet IV, which begins "Oh My Black Soul!" The poem talks about spiritual matters, such as the fear of bodily sickness as well as of death and God's disfavor, all of which he wants to escape. If he escapes his body in death, however, he will face God's displeasure. At the same time, if he stays alive, he continues to experience bodily weakness. The resolution to these fears comes when Donne embraces salvation so that he no longer has to fear sickness or dying.

One last topic that appears frequently in poems of almost every country and age is nature. The English Romantics were notable for having very movingly described mountains, country meadows, gurgling streams, glittering lakes and shady groves in their poetry. The king of English nature poetry, so to speak, was William Wordsworth (1770–1850). He did more than just describe nature in his poetry. To Wordsworth, nature was the inspiration of all great poetry, and a lessened appreciation of the powers of nature sadly meant a lessening of the poet's powers. Wordsworth also saw nature as a healer and a moral guide.

Exercise 30.1

Be able to answer the following questions orally.

1. Name some of the most common subjects of poetry.

2. What does the Latin phrase *carpe diem* mean? What Latin poet used the phrase in a poem?

3. What is the title of the most famous English poem that has *carpe diem* as its theme?

4. What kind of poem frequently has love as its topic?

5. What inspired Elizabeth Barrett Browning to write *Sonnets from the Portuguese*?

6. What Medieval poet wrote many love sonnets?

7. What English writer is famous for his love sonnets?

8. What inspired Alfred Tennyson to write one of his most respected poems, "In Memoriam"?

9. What topic does a lot of metaphysical poetry deal with? Name some of the metaphysical poets.

10. Who is the most famous nature poet of the Romantic Period? In what ways was he a "nature poet"?

THEMES AND TOPICS OF POETRY

Exercise 30.2

Write down the word in the blanks indicated by the description. The letters in the dark boxes will spell a mystery word.

1. When all three rules of rhyme are followed, the rhyme is said to be ____.
2. Rhyme does not involve the spelling of words but their ____.
3. Newspapers, essays, novels are written not in poetry, but in ____.
4. A line of poetry that contains six feet is called a ____.
5. When two words do not have the same vowel sound but the same sounds after the vowel, there is ____.
6. To ____ a poem means to determine the stress pattern and meter of a poem.
7. Consonance, assonance and identity are all imperfect ____.

1. **P** E R F E C T
2. S O **U** N D
3. **P** R O S E
4. **H** E X A M E T E R
5. C **O** N S O **N** A N C E
6. S C A **N**
7. R H **Y** M E

Using the letters in the dark boxes above, write down the mystery word and tell what it means.

E U P H O N Y

Exercise 30.3

I have a little shadow that goes in and out with me,
And what can be the use of him is more than I can see.
He is very, very like me from the heels up to the head;
And I see him jump before me, when I jump into my bed.

The funniest thing about him is the way he likes to grow—
Not at all like proper children, which is always very slow;
For he sometimes shoots up taller like an india-rubber ball,
And he sometimes gets so little that there's none of him at all.

He hasn't got a notion of how children ought to play,
And can only make a fool of me in every sort of way.
He stays so close beside me, he's a coward, you can see;
I'd think shame to stick to nursie as that shadow sticks to me!

One morning, very early, before the sun was up,
I rose and found the shining dew on every buttercup;
But my lazy little shadow, like an arrant sleepy-head,
Had stayed at home behind me and was fast asleep in bed.

Which of the following BEST describes the children's verse "My Shadow" by Robert Louis Stevenson, printed above?
a) a four-stanza trochaic heptameter verse with the rhyme scheme *aaba*
b) a four-stanza trochaic octameter verse with the rhyme scheme *aabb*
c) a four-stanza iambic pentameter verse with the rhyme scheme *aabb*
d) a four-stanza iambic hexameter verse with the rhyme scheme *aabb*
e) a four-stanza iambic heptameter verse with the rhyme scheme *aabb*

Poetry and Poetics 31
Enjambment and End Stop

> Oh! what's the matter? what's the matter?
> What is't that ails young Harry Gill?
> That evermore his teeth they chatter,
> Chatter, chatter, chatter still.

Reading the above four lines from William Wordsworth's poem Goody Blake and Harry Gill," you will notice that each line has a pause or stop at the end. *End stop*, as this kind of line is called, is the opposite of *enjambment* in which there is *no* pause or stop at the end of the line. Observe the enjambment in the lines printed below, written by John Keats.

> My heart aches, and a drowsy numbness pains
> My sense, as though of hemlock I had drunk,

You will notice that the first the two lines taken from "Ode to a Nightingale" ends in a verb—*pains* (which means "causes pain"). The object of the verb, however, is in the second line. There is no pause until the word sense in the second line, indicated by a comma. Read the sentence, and you will find out for yourself: "A drowsy numbness pains my sense." Did you notice there is no pause until the period? Because there is no pause at the end of the first line, it is said to have *enjambment*.

Exercise 31.1

Read the following statements. If the statement is false, circle *F*; if the statement is true, circle *T*.

1. (**T** or F) A literal statement means what it says.
2. (**T** or F) A metonymy is a figure of speech in which one word is used for another closely related to it.
3. (**T** or F) The statement "He cried a river of tears" contains a metaphor.
4. (T or **F**) Iambic meter has the rhythmic pattern / ⌣.
5. (T or **F**) A spondaic foot contains three syllables.
6. (**T** or F) A line of strict anapestic pentameter contains fifteen syllables.
7. (**T** or F) A line of strict dactylic trimeter has nine syllables.
8. (T or **F**) Caesura rhyme is the same as end rhyme.
9. (**T** or F) A sonnet has fourteen lines.
10. (**T** or F) A Shakespearean sonnet ends in a rhyming couplet.

ENJAMBMENT AND END STOP

Exercise 31.2

Write down the word in the blanks indicated by the description. The letters in the dark boxes will spell a mystery word.

1. A foot with the metrical pattern ᴗ / is called a(n) ____.
2. A Petrarchan sonnet is also called a(n) ____ sonnet.
3. Rhyme within a line of poetry is called ____ rhyme.
4. A foot with the metrical pattern / ᴗ is called a(n) ____ foot.
5. An ____ is a line of poetry that has eight feet.
6. When two-syllable words that are not iambic rhyme, it is ____ rhyme.

1. I A **M** B
2. **I** T A L I A N
3. I N T E R N A **L**
4. **T** R O C H A I C
5. **O** C T A M E T E R
6. F E M I **N** I N E

Using the letters in the dark boxes above, write down the mystery word and tell what it means.

M I L T O N

Exercise 31.3

The boy stood on the burning deck,
    Whence all but him had fled;
The flame that lit the battle's wreck
    Shone round him o'er the dead.

Yet beautiful and bright he stood,
    As born to rule the storm;
A creature of heroic blood,
    A proud though childlike form.

The flames rolled on—he would not go
    Without his father's word;
That father, faint in death below,
    His voice no longer heard.

He called aloud, "Say, father, say
    If yet my task is done?"
He knew not that the chieftain lay
    Unconscious of his son.

"Speak, father!" once again he cried,
    "If I may yet be gone!"
And but the booming shots replied,
    And fast the flames rolled on.

Upon his brow he felt their breath,
    And in his waving hair;
And looked from that lone post of death
    In still, yet brave despair.

And shouted but once more aloud
    "My father! must I stay?"
While o'er him fast, through sail and shroud,
    The wreathing fires made way.

ENJAMBMENT AND END STOP

They wrapped the ship in splendor wild,
  They caught the flag on high,
And streamed above the gallant child
  Like banners in the sky.

Then came a burst of thunder sound—
  The boy—oh! where was he?
—Ask of the winds that far around
  With fragments strew the sea;

With mast, and helm, and pennon fair.
  That well had borne their part—
But the noblest thing that perished there
  Was that young, faithful heart.

Which of the following BEST describes the poem "Casabianca" by Felicia Heman, printed above?

a) a ten-stanza trochaic tetrameter and trimeter narrative poem with the rhyme scheme *aabb*

b) a ten-stanza trochaic tetrameter and trimeter narrative poem with the rhyme scheme *abab*

c) a ten-stanza iambic tetrameter and trimeter ballad with the rhyme scheme *aabb*

d) a ten-stanza iambic tetrameter and trimeter ballad with the rhyme scheme *abab*

e) a ten-stanza iambic pentameter and tetrameter elegy with the rhyme scheme *abab*

Poetry and Poetics 32
Middle Ages and Renaissance

The poetry of the early Middle Ages (before 1100) was written in Old English. The term *Old English* does not mean that the English is old. The term rather separates it from two other kinds of English—*Middle English* and *Modern English*. Although Shakespeare's English seems old to most readers, it is not Old English; it is Modern English! Old English is a kind of German, as the people who spoke it in England had come from what is now Germany. Modern readers can recognize some words, but in many ways, it is like a foreign language. There are even letters that are not in modern English: the aesc (æ—pronounced "ash"), thorn (þ) and eth (ð). See the passage below, taken from the first lines of the Old English poem *Beowulf*.

> Hwæt! we Gar-Dena   in gear-dagum
> þeod-cyninga   þrym gefrunon,
> hu þa æðelingas   ellen fremedon.
> Oft Scyld Scefing   sceaðena þreatum,
> monegum mægðum   meodo-setla ofteah.

You can notice several things about Old English poetry from this passage. First, the lines are divided in the middle. Second, there is a lot of alliteration. (Notice the repetition of beginning letters in each line.) A third characteristic, which you cannot tell from the passage, is that Old English poetry used metaphors known as *kennings*. One example of a kenning is the use of the word *whale-road* in *Beowulf* for ocean.

The first known poet of the Middle Ages was a man named Cædmon. What is so unusual about this poet is that even though he had no talent for poetry, or even formal training in it, he wrote beautiful poems. Apparently, too, he was not a man of letters—his job was herding pigs. How did Cædmon, then, become a great poet of the Middle Ages? The Medieval historian Bede gives us the answer in a story. At a feast, the harp was being passed around for guests to sing a poem. Em-

MIDDLE AGES AND RENAISSANCE

barrassed that he himself could not sing, Cædmon left the feast and went to a stable where he lay down to sleep. There he had a dream. A man appeared to him and said, "Sing me a song." Cædmon said that he did not have a song to sing. He could not compose poetry. The man insisted, and told him sing a song about creation. Cædmon did as he was told and when he woke up, he remembered the poem and sang it to others, who deemed it a miracle and a gift from God. You can read the poem that Cædmon "wrote" today—but none of his other poems. Unfortunately, only this one poem about creation has survived.

Another poem written in the early Middle Ages—and the most famous—is *Beowulf*. It is about the exploits of the great warrior from an area in Sweden called Geatland. In a previous section you learned how Beowulf bravely fought against monsters and performed superhuman feats. The poem, although more than a thousand years old, was only recently discovered in the 1800s. When scholars read it for the first time, they thought there really wasn't much to it. However, J. R. R. Tolkien, an Oxford professor and author of *Lord of the Rings* and the *Hobbit*, surprised them with an essay titled "*Beowulf*: The Monster and the Critics." In the essay Tolkien said that *Beowulf* was a lot more complex than they thought it was. He explained how it was a worthy work of imaginative literature, not just exciting folklore.

In the later Middle Ages (1100–1450), one work stands out among all others. It is the collection of poems titled *Canterbury Tales*, written by Geoffrey Chaucer (1340–1400). In this work there are many serious and funny stories told in rhyming couplets. A couplet, you have already learned, is a stanza of two lines. A rhyming couplet is two lines of poetry with end rhyme. The work was written in Middle English, which is easier to read than Old English, for sure, but too difficult for many modern readers. The best way to describe Chaucer's long work is that it is a *satire*. If you do not understand this about it, you will miss many of the ideas that Chaucer is trying to communicate as well as much of its humor. A satirical poem is one that pokes fun at something or somebody for a serious purpose. It is not malicious; rather it tries to point out some flaw or bad thing in society or people so that it can be corrected for the benefit of everyone. Chaucer mostly points out the evil ways of the monks, friars and other religious people of the day, who seemed, to Chaucer at least, to care more about money than the poor. He does it in such a way, though, it makes the reader laugh.

The poet that dominates the Renaissance Period is the much often quoted William Shakespeare (1564–1616). There were other poets of the period, some of them have already been mentioned, but because of the depth and beauty of his poetry, Shakespeare has remained a favorite. Passages of Shakespeare's poetry have been quoted so often that, they have entered the English language as idioms. You might not be familiar with these idioms, or expressions, but many adults are, such as *to the manner born* and *sweets to the sweet*, which are both quotations from his play *Hamlet*.

Exercise 32.1

Read the following statements. If the statement is false, circle *F*; if the statement is true, circle *T*.

1. (**T** or F)   William Shakespeare's plays were written in Modern English.

2. (**T** or F)   The writer of *The Hobbit* thought that the Old English poem *Beowulf* was good literature.

3. (T or **F**)   The *Canterbury Tales* is a collection of Petrarchan sonnets.

4. (T or **F**)   Geoffrey Chaucer wrote the *Canterbury Tales* in Modern English.

5. (T or **F**)   *Beowulf* was written by the poet Cædmon.

MIDDLE AGES AND RENAISSANCE

Exercise 32.2

Write down the word in the blanks indicated by the description. The letters in the dark boxes will spell a mystery word.

1. ____ wrote the most praised Middle English work of the later Medieval Period.

2. ____ is a Latin phrase that means "seize the day" and it is used to identify poetry that has the theme of making the best use of time.

3. Beowulf was a hero who came from ____ to help the Danish king Hrothgar.

4. When there is a pause or stop at the end of a line, the line is said to have ____.

5. Andrew ____ was a metaphysical poet.

6. A lyric poem that deals with a serious topic is called an ____.

7. ____ wrote an essay showing that *Beowulf* had literary value.

1. C H A U C E R
2. C A R P E D I E M
3. G E A T L A N D
4. E N D S T O P
5. M A R V E L L
6. O D E
7. T O L K I E N

Using the letters in the dark boxes above, write down the mystery word and tell what it means.

Exercise 32.3

> The man who wants a garden fair,
>   Or small or very big,
> With flowers growing here and there,
>   Must bend his back and dig.
>
> The things are mighty few on earth
>   That wishes can attain.
> Whate'er we want of any worth
>   We've got to work to gain.
>
> It matters not what goal you seek,
>   Its secret here reposes:
> You've got to dig from week to week
>   To get Results or Roses.

Which of the following BEST describes the theme and structure of the poem "Results and Roses" by Edgar A. Guest, printed above?
a) This ballad stanza poem is about diligence.
b) This iambic tetrameter poem is about diligence.
c) This trochaic tetrameter and trimeter poem is about death.
d) This iambic pentameter poem is about beauty.
e) This ballad stanza ode is about beauty.

Poetry and Poetics 33
The Romantic Period

Writers are influenced by the period that they live in. The poets of the Romantic Period (discussed in "The Destruction of Sennacherib") were living in an age of great turmoil. There were revolutions, or great changes, in the way people lived and they way in which they were ruled or governed. There was the Industrial Revolution, a time when machines started taking the place of people. Then there was the American Revolution and the French Revolution, in which the rights of the common people were voiced. The Romantic Period writers reacted to these revolutions in interesting ways. People wanted to throw away the artificial things of the world, like a class system that said that rich people were better than poor people. They also wanted to get back to nature—the way we were originally created—where people were equal and there were no polluting factories. One Frenchman of this period, named Jean Jacque Rousseau, was bold enough to say if it wasn't natural, it wasn't good. European society, he said was bad because it was artificial—despite its many great accomplishments in printing books, ship-making and other technologies. He praised the simple living of the native peoples of America because they were *natural*. He called them "noble savages."

If there is one thing that characterizes the Romantic Period, then, it is being natural—including the way that poetry was written. The "spokesman" for the Romantic Period, William Wordsworth in his Preface to *Lyrical Ballads* said that poems had to read the way that people really spoke. How often do common people naturally speak of Phoebus or Apollo? Not often. So, then, it should not be used in poetry. Wordsworth chose to write about common people—not kings and queens—because they were natural. They did not pretend and act more important than they were, as "rich" folks did, and so emotions could be better expressed through their speech.

Part of this get-back-to-nature movement also involved descriptions of nature in poetry. There are wonderfully beautiful descriptions of nature in Romantic Period poems, such as "This Lime Tree, My Prison Bower," written by Samuel Taylor Coleridge (1772–1834). In the poem, Coleridge describes the beauties of nature that his friends could see, but he could not, as he was "imprisoned" under lime tree, having injured his leg. However, Coleridge was still able to enjoy the wonders of the natural world just where he was sitting beneath the tree:

> Pale beneath the blaze
> Hung the transparent foliage; and I watched
> Some broad and sunny leaf, and loved to see
> The shadow of the leaf and stem above
> Dappling its sunshine! And that walnut-tree
> Was richly tinged, and a deep radiance lay
> Full on the ancient ivy, which usurps
> Those fronting elms, and now, with blackest mass
> Makes their dark branches gleam a lighter hue
> Through the late twilight: and though now the bat
> Wheels silent by, and not a swallow twitters,
> Yet still the solitary humble-bee
> Sings in the bean-flower! Henceforth I shall know
> That Nature ne'er deserts the wise and pure.

Other poets of the Romantic period besides those already mentioned in this section—John Keats, Percy Bysshe Shelley, and John Clare—also wrote lush descriptions of nature. Much of the Romantic poetry is still read today because the beauties it talks about are timeless. Also, in general it is much easier to read than the poetry of earlier periods, especially the poetry of William Wordsworth and John Clare.

On the opposite side of the Atlantic Ocean, American poets echoed the style and subjects of the English poets, including lush descriptions of nature. The most popular American poets of the 1800s were called Fireside Poets and included Oliver Wendell Holmes, James Russell Lowell, John Greenleaf Whittier, and Henry Wadsworth Longfellow.

THE ROMANTIC PERIOD

Much of the poetry written in America during this time imitated the great poets in England. However, they did find at times a distinctive voice. Longfellow became the most popular of them all, and made American, not British, things the topic of his most popular and greatest poems. *Evangeline*, for example, takes place in the New World, not the Old. *The Courtship of Miles Standish* is about the Pilgrims, and there are few subjects more American than the Pilgrims. And *Hiawatha* is about the native Americans.

Exercise 33.1

Be able to answer the following questions orally.

1. What was the Industrial Revolution?
2. What peculiar idea did the Frenchman Jacque Rousseau have regarding nature and civilization?
3. Name at least two characteristics of Romantic Period Literature.
4. Name three Romantic Period poets.
5. Who were the Fireside Poets?

Exercise 33.2

Write down the word in the blanks indicated by the description. The letters in the dark boxes will spell a mystery word.

1. The words *dapper* and *wrapper* have ____ rhyme.
2. A ____ is a pause inside a line of poetry.
3. A Petrarchan sonnet is also called an ____ sonnet.
4. A line of poetry that has eight feet is called octameter; an *animal* with eight feet is called an ____.
5. A poem that tells a story is called a ____ poem.
6. The Quaker John Greenleaf ____ was one of the Fireside Poets.

POETRY & POETICS 33

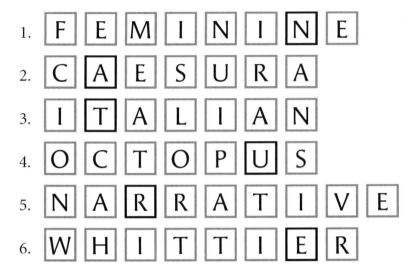

Using the letters in the dark boxes above, write down the mystery word and explain what it has to do with poetry.

Exercise 33.3

Just in the gray of the dawn, as the mists uprose from the meadows,
There was a stir and a sound in the slumbering village of Plymouth;
Clanging and clicking of arms, and the order imperative, "Forward!"
Given in tone suppressed, a tramp of feet, and then silence.

Which of the following BEST describes the above lines taken from the poem "The Courtship of Miles Standish" by Henry Wadsworth Longfellow, printed above?
a) anapestic hexameter with the last foot a trochee
b) anapestic hexameter with the last foot an iamb
c) blank verse with alliteration in the second, third and fourth lines
d) dactylic heptameter with a metonymy in the second line
e) dactylic hexameter with the last foot a trochee and with a metonymy in the second line

Poetry and Poetics 34
Victorian and Modern Poets

You learned in the previous section that what defined the Romantic Period was change, or revolution. Much of those changes, however, were not fully felt until the Victorian Period. One of the changes involved faith. Old beliefs were being challenged on all fronts in the Victorian Period. These beliefs were challenged by new ways of thinking as well as by science. New thinkers said that the Bible could not be trusted. And in his book *Origin of Species*, Charles Darwin suggested that man was not created but evolved from a lower order of animal. One famous Victorian poet, named Matthew Arnold (1822–1888), showed this challenge to faith in a poem titled "Dover Beach." In the poem, Arnold compares faith to a sea. Once the sea went round the earth, but now it has gone back with the tide, and can hardly be heard. He was saying, in other words, that faith was disappearing from the modern world.

> The Sea of Faith
> Was once, too, at the full, and round earth's shore
> Lay like the folds of a bright girdle furled.
> But now I only hear
> Its melancholy, long, withdrawing roar,
> Retreating, to the breath
> Of the night-wind, down the vast edges drear
> And naked shingles of the world.

The "giant" of the Victorian Poet was the poet Alfred Tennyson, who was greatly honored in his own time. He was elected poet laureate after the death of William Wordsworth in 1850, and later made a baron. Often you will hear Tennyson referred to as *Lord* Tennyson. Tennyson also wrote about declining faith and increasing doubt in the world in his work *Idylls of the King*.

There were poets, however, such as Christina Rossetti (1830–1894) and Girard Manley Hopkins (1844–1889), that were religious and who voiced deep, personal devotion. Rossetti's poetry, often sad, speaks of suffering in the world and of a desire to be closer with her Lord. Gerard

Manley Hopkins' poetry melded nature with faith. In nature he saw God the Father in spotted cows, fish and skies with floating clouds; he saw the crucified Christ in the flying of a bird of prey; and saw the Holy Spirit in ground seemingly wasted by men's tilling the ground. Other major poets of the Victorian Period include Robert Browning, his wife Elizabeth Barrett, and Rudyard Kipling.

Although William Butler Yeats (1865–1939) and Thomas Hardy (1840–1928) lived and wrote during the Victorian Period, their poetry was mostly written in the twentieth century—the Modern Period. Thomas Hardy is probably the only great novelist who was also equally talented in writing poetry. He is considered one of the greatest novelists of all time as well as one of the greatest poets of the twentieth century. Thomas Hardy's *Satires of Circumstance* in 1914 includes poems that are very different from the poems of Rossetti and Hopkins. "The Convergence of the Twain," for example, suggests there is no meaning in what happens to us in the world and therefore there is no comfort to be had when bad things happen. The poem says in so many words that we are victims of "blind" fate. Other great British poets of the modern period include A. E. Houseman, W. H. Auden and T. S. Eliot.

Two of the greatest American poets of the nineteenth and twentieth centuries were Emily Dickinson (1830–1886) and Robert Frost (1874–1963). Emily Dickinson was the daughter of an important lawyer. Dickinson never married, but lived in her family house her entire life, separate from the world. Her poetry was as unknown to the outside world as was. Only seven of her one thousand poems were published in her lifetime. Yet, she is undoubtedly a writer of great genius. Her poems are usually quite short, but deal deftly with hard topics, such as faith, love and death.

Like Emily Dickinson, Robert Frost was also an outsider, so to speak. Although he did not lock himself away from the world in the same way Dickinson had, he did not have family, connections or money to promote himself. He worked hard to earn a living and hard at his poetry, which was eventually published in 1913 while he was in England. Robert Frost's poetry uses vivid images to create quaint pictures of New England life. Throughout the years, readers have found Frost's

VICTORIAN AND MODERN POETS

talk about walls, apple trees, and gardens as well as his Yankee, "homey" style of writing very appealing. Yet the poems are very suggestive; in other words. In one poem, titled "Stopping by the Woods on a Snowy Evening," for example, Frost talks about a lonely ride out through the woods in a sleigh, and yet when readers finish the poem, they suspect it means something other than what it appears to be about.

Exercise 34.1

Be able to answer the following questions orally.

1. Who wrote "Dover Beach" and what does the poem talk about? How does the poem serve as a kind of "mirror" of the Victorian Period?

2. Who was the "giant" poet of the Victorian Period? Name one of his greatest works.

3. What Victorian poets talked about their devotion to God?

4. What famous English writer was equally good as a poet as a novelist? Did he write during the Victorian or Modern Period?

5. Who were the two "giant" American poets of nineteenth and twentieth centuries?

Exercise 34.2

Write down the word in the blanks indicated by the description.

1. The first syllable of the word *barrel* is ____.

2. George Herbert's "Easter Wings" is a ____ poem.

3. Two clashing words put together are called an ____.

4. ____ is a poet that did not use normal capitalization in his poetry and did not even capitalize his name.

5. The ____ fallacy is a lot like personification in that it gives human traits to nonhuman things.

6. Verbal irony is also called ____, especially when spoken.

POETRY & POETICS 34

7. Many idioms come from Shakespeare's plays; the two idioms *sweets to the sweet* and *to the manner born* come from ____.

8. William Butler ____ was a poet who lived during the Victorian and Modern Period.

9. The extremely popular poet Alfred Tennyson was made a ____.

10. ____ was a poet of the Modern Period.

11. Though only seven of her one thousand poems had been published in her lifetime, ____ Dickinson is one of the most famous American poets of the nineteenth century.

1. S **T** R E S S E D
2. S **H** A P E
3. **O** X Y M O R O N
4. C U **M** M I N G S
5. P **A** T H E T I C
6. **S** A R C A S M
7. **H** A M L E T
8. Y E **A** T S
9. B A **R** O N
10. H A **R** D Y
11. E M I L **Y**

Copy the mystery word and tell what it means.

T H O M A S H A R D Y

VICTORIAN AND MODERN POETS

Exercise 34.3

> Once there was a little boy,
> With curly hair and pleasant eye—
> A boy who always told the truth,
> And never, never told a lie.
>
> And when he trotted off to school,
> The children all about would cry,
> "There goes the curly-headed boy—
> The boy that never tells a lie."
>
> And everybody loved him so,
> Because he always told the truth,
> That every day, as he grew up,
> 'Twas said, "There goes the honest youth."
>
> And when the people that stood near
> Would turn to ask the reason why,
> The answer would be always this:
> "Because he never tells a lie."

Which of the following BEST describes the anonymous verse "The Boy Who Never Told a Lie," printed above?
a) iambic tetrameter with the rhyme scheme *abac*
b) iambic tetrameter with the rhyme scheme *abcb*
c) ballad stanza with the rhyme scheme *abcb*
d) trochaic tetrameter with the rhyme scheme *abac*
e) trochaic pentameter with the rhyme scheme *abcb*

Poetry and Poetics 35
Writing Poetry

Is writing poetry hard work? It most certainly is! William Wordsworth described poetry as a spontaneous flow of powerful feelings. At least one poem, in fact, he apparently *did* write spontaneously—quickly and without reworking—and that was his "Idiot Boy." But if you read his sister Dorothy's journals, you will get the idea that Wordsworth worked very hard at writing his poems. In one journal entry Dorothy writes that her brother "composed without much success at the sheepfold," and in another that he "could not compose much" and that he "fatigued himself [made himself tired] with altering [changing what he wrote]."

There is not one way to write a poem. There isn't even any one way to *begin* writing a poem. William Wordsworth, for example, begin writing one of his poems ("The Idiot Boy") with the one line that had been told to him by a friend. Edgar Allen Poe said that he began his poem "The Raven" with one *letter*. Whatever the case may be, certainly these authors began with an idea, or the poem could never progress. There are many things to consider, too, when beginning a poem, such as the form that it will take. Will it be a sonnet or an ode? Will it be written in free verse—verse with no regular meter? Or will it be blank verse?

To make writing your own poem easier, you will be given the process and form of the poem. When you get practice, however, you will devise your own method.

Exercise 35.1

Follow the steps in writing a poem. You may need assistance from a teacher or other adult.

- Think of something that happened to you that is exciting to tell and write it down on paper.

- Divide the story up into equal parts. The parts may be as few as five and as many as nine. These parts will become your stanzas.

- Write the parts in *ballad stanza*. The first and third lines of ballad stanza, you will remember, are iambic tetrameter, while the second and fourth lines are iambic trimeter.

- Attempt to have the second and fourth lines rhyme.

Poetry and Poetics 36
Review

Exercise 36.1

Match the word in the left-hand column with its definition in the right-hand column.

a) oxymoron

b) synecdoche

c) stanza

d) scop

e) iamb

f) pattern poetry

g) metaphor

h) metonymy

i) scansion

j) verbal irony

__f__ 1. another word for a shape poem

__c__ 2. the "paragraph" of a poem

__g__ 3. a figure of speech that makes a comparison

__b__ 4. a figure of speech in which a part represents the whole, or the whole represents a part

__h__ 5. a figure of speech in which a word is used for another closely associated to it

__j__ 6. a figure of speech in which what is expressed is opposite to what is meant

__a__ 7. clashing words put together

__d__ 8. an English poet and singer of the early Middle Ages

__i__ 9. reading through a poem for its meter

__e__ 10. a foot with the syllable pattern ⌣ /

REVIEW

Exercise 36.2

Match the word in the left-hand column with its definition in the right-hand column.

a) enjambment

b) dactylic

c) spondee

d) blank verse

e) caesura

f) trochee

g) catalectic

h) free verse

i) anapestic

j) heptameter

_f_ 1. a foot with the syllable pattern / ⌣

_c_ 2. a foot with the syllable pattern / /

_g_ 3. a line of poetry which ends in an imperfect or incomplete foot

_d_ 4. describing a kind of poem that is made up of lines of unrhymed iambic pentameter

_h_ 5. describing a kind of poem that has no regular stress pattern

_e_ 6. a pause or break in the line of a poem

_a_ 7. the technique when a line of poetry runs into the next line without a pause

_j_ 8. a line of poetry containing seven feet

_i_ 9. a foot with the syllable pattern ⌣ ⌣ /

_b_ 10. a foot with the syllable pattern / ⌣ ⌣

Exercise 36.3

Match the word in the left-hand column with its definition in the right-hand column.

a) apostrophe

b) *carpe diem*

c) literal

d) personification

e) poet

f) metaphysical poet

g) foot

h) elegy

i) ode

j) lyric

__e__ 1. Like the word *scop*, the meaning of this word in its original language means "to make."

__f__ 2. a term invented by the dictionary maker Samuel Johnson to describe poets who are spiritual

__h__ 3. a funeral poem

__d__ 4. giving human traits to nonhuman things

__c__ 5. meaning exactly what is said

__i__ 6. a formal lyric poem about a serious topic

__j__ 7. a personal poem that talks about inner feelings

__g__ 8. a unit of syllables in a line of poetry

__b__ 9. "Make good use of time, as it passes very quickly"

__a__ 10. a figure of speech in which the speaker of a poem addresses an idea (such as Liberty) or a person who is not present

WORKS CONSULTED

Allison, Alexander W., et al., editors. *The Norton Anthology of Poetry*. Revised Shorter Edition. New York: W. W. Norton & Company, 1975.

Ansley, Clarke F., editor. *The Columbia Encyclopedia*. New York: P. F. Collier and Son, 1935.

Bridgewater, William and Seymour Kurtz, editors. *The Columbia Encyclopedia*. 3rd ed. New York: Columbia University Press, 1963.

Gove, Philip Babcock, editor. *Webster's Third New International Dictionary*. Springfield, Massachusetts: Merriam-Webster, 2003.

Heaney, Seamus. *Beowulf*. New York: W. W. Norton & Company, 2000.

Moore, Samuel. *The Elements of Old English*. Anne Arbor, Michigan: The George Wahr Publishing Company, 1977.

Morris, William, editor. *American Heritage Dictionary of the English Language*. Boston: Houghton Mifflin, 1981.

Preminger, Alex and T. V. F. Brogan. The New Princeton Encyclopedia of Poetry and Poetics. New York: Princeton University Press, 1993.

Wood, Clement. *The Rhyming Dictionary*. Garden City, New York: Doubleday and Company, 1936.

Typeset
using X͟ǝLATEX
in 13-point Minion
with notes & headings
in Angie Sans

Made in the USA
Columbia, SC
01 October 2022